THE KURDS

THE KURDS

LeeAnne Gelletly

Mason Crest
Philadelphia

Mason Crest
450 Parkway Drive, Suite D
Broomall, PA 19008
www.masoncrest.com

Printed and bound in the United States of America.

CPSIA Compliance Information: Batch #MNMME2016.
For further information, contact Mason Crest at 1-866-MCP-Book.

  3 5 7 9 8 6 4 2

Library of Congress Cataloging-in-Publication Data
        on file at the Library of Congress

        978-1-4222-3454-9 (hc)
        978-1-4222-8447-6 (ebook)

Major Nations of the Modern Middle East series ISBN: 978-1-4222-3438-9

TABLE OF CONTENTS

MAJOR NATIONS OF THE MODERN MIDDLE EAST

Afghanistan	Lebanon
Egypt	Pakistan
Iran	The Palestinians
Iraq	Saudi Arabia
Israel	Syria
Jordan	Turkey
The Kurds	

KEY ICONS TO LOOK FOR:

 Words to Understand: These words with their easy-to-understand definitions will increase the reader's understanding of the text, while building vocabulary skills.

 Sidebars: This boxed material within the main text allows readers to build knowledge, gain insights, explore possibilities, and broaden their perspectives by weaving together additional information to provide realistic and holistic perspectives.

 Research Projects: Readers are pointed toward areas of further inquiry connected to each chapter. Suggestions are provided for projects that encourage deeper research and analysis.

 Text-Dependent Questions: These questions send the reader back to the text for more careful attention to the evidence presented there.

 Series Glossary of Key Terms: This back-of-the book glossary contains terminology used throughout this series. Words found here increase the reader's ability to read and comprehend higher-level books and articles in this field.

Introduction

by Camille Pecastaing, Ph.D.

Oil shocks, wars, terrorism, nuclear proliferation, military and autocratic regimes, ethnic and religious violence, riots and revolutions are the most frequent headlines that draw attention to the Middle East. The region is also identified with Islam, often in unflattering terms. The creed is seen as intolerant and illiberal, oppressive of women and minorities. There are concerns that violence is not only endemic in the region, but also follows migrants overseas. All clichés contain a dose of truth, but that truth needs to be placed in its proper context. The turbulences visited upon the Middle East that grab the headlines are only the symptoms of a deep social phenomenon: the demographic transition. This transition happens once in the life of a society. It is the transition from the agrarian to the industrial age, from rural to urban life, from illiteracy to mass education, all of which supported by massive population growth. It is this transition that fueled the recent development of East Asia, leading to rapid social and economic modernization and to some form of democratization there. It is the same transition that, back in the 19th century, inspired nationalism and socialism in Europe, and that saw the excesses of imperialism, fascism, and Marxist-Leninism. The demographic transition is a period of high risks and great opportunities, and the challenge for the Middle East is to fall on the right side of the sword.

In 1950, the population of the Middle East was about 100 million; it passed 250 million in 1990. Today it exceeds 400 million, to reach about 700 million by 2050. The growth of urbanization is rapid, and concentrated on the coasts and along the few rivers. 1950 Cairo, with an estimated population of 2.5 million, grew into Greater Cairo, a metropolis of about 18 million people. In the same period, Istanbul went from one to 14 million. This expanding populace was bound to test the social system, but regimes were unwilling to take chances with the private sector, reserving for the state a prominent place in the economy. That model failed, population grew faster than the economy, and stress fractures already appeared in the 1970s, with recurrent riots following IMF adjustment programs and the emergence of radical Islamist movements. Against a backdrop of military coups and social unrest, regimes consolidated their rule by subsidizing basic commodities, building up patronage networks (with massive under-employment in a non-productive public sector), and cementing autocratic practices. Decades of continuity in political elites between 1970 and 2010 gave the impression that they had succeeded. The Arab spring shattered that illusion.

The Arab spring exposed a paradox that the Middle East was both one, yet also diverse. Arab unity was apparent in the contagion: societies inspired other societies in a revolutionary wave that engulfed the region yet remained exclusive to it. The rebellious youth was the same; it watched the same footage on al Jazeera and turned to the same online social networks. The claims were the same: less corruption, less police abuse, better standards of living, and off with the tyrants. In some cases, the struggle was one: Syria became a global battlefield, calling young fighters from all around the region to a common cause. But there were differences in the way states fared during the Arab spring. Some escaped unscathed; some got by with a burst of public spending or a sprinkling of democratic reforms, and others yet collapsed into civil wars. The differential resilience of the regimes owes to both the strength and cohesiveness of the repressive apparatus, and the depth of the fiscal cushion they could tap into to buy social peace. Yemen, with a GDP per capita of $4000 and Qatar, at $94,000, are not the same animal. It also became apparent that, despite shared frustrations and a common cause, protesters and insurgents were extremely diverse.

Some embraced free-market capitalism, while others clamored for state welfare to provide immediate improvements to their standards of living. Some thought in terms of country, while other questioned that idea. The day after the Arab spring, everyone looked to democracy for solutions, but few were prepared to invest in the grind of democratic politics. It also quickly became obvious that the competition inherent in democratic life would tear at the social fabric. The few experiments with free elections exposed the formidable polarization between Islamists and non-Islamists. Those modern cleavages paralleled ancient but pregnant divisions. Under the Ottoman Millet system, ethnic and sectarian communities had for centuries coexisted in relative, self-governed segregation. Those communities remained a primary feature of social life, and in a dense, urbanized environment, fractures between Christians and Muslims, Shi'as and Sunnis, Arabs and Berbers, Turks and Kurds were combustible. Autocracy had kept the genie of divisiveness in the bottle. Democracy unleashed it.

This does not mean democracy has to forever elude the region, but that in countries where the state concentrates both political and economic power, elections are a polarizing zero-sum game—even more so when public patronage has to be cut back because of chronic budget deficits. The solution is to bring some distance between the state and the national economy. If all goes well, a growing private sector would absorb the youth, and generate taxes to balance state budgets. For that, the Middle East needs just enough democracy to mitigate endemic corruption, to protect citizens from abuse and extortion, and to allow greater transparency over public finances and over licensing to crony privateers.

Better governance is necessary but no sufficient. The region still needs to figure out a developmental model and find its niche in the global economy. Unfortunately, the timing is not favorable. Mature economies are slow growing, and emerging markets in Asia and Africa are generally more competitive than the Middle East. To succeed, the region has to leverage its assets, starting with its geographic location between Europe, Africa, and Asia. Regional businesses and governments are looking to anchor themselves in south-south relationships. They see the potential clientele of hundreds of millions in Africa and South Asia reaching middle class status, many of whom Muslim. The Middle East can also count on its vast sources of energy, and on the capital accumulated during years of high oil prices. Financial investments in specific sectors, like transport, have already made local companies like Emirates Airlines and DP World global players.

With the exception of Turkey and Israel, the weakness is human capital, which is either unproductive for lack of adequate education, or uncompetitive, because wage expectations in the region are relatively higher than in other emerging economies. The richer Arab countries have worked around the problem by importing low-skilled foreign labor—immigrants who notoriously toil for little pay and even less protection. In parallel, they have made massive investments in higher education, so that the productivity of their native workforce eventually reaches the compensations they expect. For lack of capital, the poorer Arab countries could not follow that route. Faced with low capitalization, sticky wages and high unemployment, they have instead allowed a shadow economy to grow. The arrangement keeps people employed, if at low levels of productivity, and in a manner that brings no tax revenue to the state.

Overall, the commerce of the region with the rest of the world is unhealthy. Oil exporters tend to be one-product economies highly vulnerable to fluctuations in global prices. Labor-rich countries depend too much on remittances from workers in the European Union and the oil-producing countries of the Gulf. Some of the excess labor has found employment in the jihadist sector, a high-risk but up and coming industry which pays decent salaries. For the poorer states of the region, jihadists are the ticket to foreign strategic rent. The Middle East got a taste for it in the early days of the Cold War, when either superpower provided aid to those who declared themselves in their camp. Since then, foreign strategic rent has come in many forms: direct military aid, preferential trade agreements, loan guarantees, financial assistance, or aid programs to cater to refugee populations. Rent never amounts to more than a few percentage points of GDP, but it is often enough to keep entrenched regimes in power. Dysfunction becomes self-perpetuating: pirates and jihadists, famine and refugees, all bear promises of aid to come from concerned distant powers. Reforms lose their urgency.

Turkey and Israel have a head start on the path to modernization and economic maturity, but they are, like the rest of the Middle East, consumed in high stakes politics that hinder their democratic life. Rather than being models that would lift others, they are virtually outliers disconnected from the rest of the region. The clock is ticking for the Middle East. The window of opportunity from the demographic transition will eventually close. Fertility is already dropping, and as the current youth bulge ages it will become a burden on the economy. The outlook for capital is also bleak. Oil is already running out for the smaller producers, all the while global prices are pushed downwards by the exploitation of new sources. The Middle East has a real possibility to break the patterns of the past, but the present is when the transition should occur.

The mountainous region historically known as Kurdistan covers parts of four modern Middle Eastern countries—Iran, Iraq, Syria, and Turkey.

Place in the World

I n the mountainous regions of Southwest Asia and the Middle East lives the largest ethnic group without a nation of its own— the Kurdish people. The Kurds number more than 25 million, which makes them the fourth-largest **ethnic** faction in the region (after Arabs, Persians, and Turks). Yet the land they consider their ancestral homeland—Kurdistan—is not recognized by the rest of the world as a separate, independent state. Instead, most of Kurdistan, which is Arabic for "land of the Kurds," is divided up among several countries, including Turkey, Iraq, Syria, and Iran.

About half of the estimated Kurdish population (14.7 million people) lives in Turkey. Around 8.8 million Kurds live in Iran, 4.9–6.5 million live in Iraq, and less than 1.7 million live in Syria. Smaller numbers can be found living in parts of the former Soviet Union (Armenia, Azerbaijan, Georgia, Turkmenistan, and Kazakhstan), while an estimated 5 million Kurds have left the region and settled in other countries, including the United States, Germany, France, and Sweden.

WHO ARE THE KURDS?

The Kurds are an ancient people who can trace their history back for thousands of years. For centuries they lived as **nomads** in the mountains of Southwest Asia, migrating with the seasons to find pastureland for their herds of livestock. In the summer, Kurdish shepherds would drive their flocks of sheep and goats into the high mountain peaks and **plateaus** of Kurdistan, while in the winter they would bring the flocks and herds down to graze in the lowlands. Since around the seventh century, the word Kurd has meant "nomad."

Most Kurds belonged to clans, tribes, and tribal confederations that claimed rights to or ownership of the land used during these seasonal migrations. Almost 800 different tribes and subtribes can be found in Kurdistan, many with their own distinct dress, music, and folklore. However, today few Kurds are nomadic. Most are farmers who have settled in villages and towns. And some have migrated to cities in search of jobs.

Kurds speak their own language, Kurdish. However, because the language exists in a variety of dialects, people from different parts of Kurdistan sometimes cannot understand one another. Most follow the **Sunni** Muslim faith, but their loyalties to their clans and tribal

Word to Understand in This Chapter

autonomous—separate and under self rule, but not necessarily independent.
ethnic—relating to a group of people who identify with one another on the basis of cultural and/or biological similarities.
nomad—a person who has not settled in one location but moves from place to place seasonally and within a certain territory.
peshmerga—Kurdish guerrilla or independence fighters.
plateau—a relatively flat land area located at a high altitude.
Sunnis—followers of the majority sect of Islam; they believe that the first four caliphs were the rightful spiritual and political leaders of Islam.

chiefs have been known to take precedence over their religious ties.

The Kurds are a fiercely independent mountain people who take great pride in their history, culture, and traditions.

THE KURDISH QUESTION

Although the Kurds' mountainous homeland never officially existed as a nation, during the late 19th century maps of Southwest Asia often identified the region of Kurdistan. After World War I (1914–18), Kurdistan stopped appearing on official maps as postwar settlements resulted in the division of Kurdish land among the modern-day countries of Turkey, Iraq, Iran, Syria, and the Soviet Union. In each country, despite their large numbers, the Kurds became a minority ethnic group.

Many Kurds did not want to be a part of another nation. The newly imposed borders separated Kurdish tribes and even families. As the new countries enforced their boundaries, tribes could no longer easily travel from one part of Kurdistan to another, and these restrictions disrupted their traditional, nomadic way of life.

In addition, the new governments often refused to acknowledge the Kurds as a separate ethnic group, or they treated them as second-class citizens by withholding basic civil and political rights. In some cases the Kurds' native language—in spoken and written form—was outlawed. Kurds were often not allowed to vote, own property, or receive an education in their own language. As a result of this repression, many Kurds found themselves shackled to a life of extreme poverty.

As the Kurdish people chafed under oppressive rule, some dreamt of forming their own separate Kurdish nation. Kurdish uprisings began in 1919, even before Kurdistan was officially divided among the four nations of Turkey, Iraq, Iran, and Syria. However, the governments of these countries quickly repressed any instances of unrest through legislation and force. In the face of government opposition, resistance continued throughout the rest of the 20th century as Kurds sporadically rose up against the authorities of their respective governments.

Most rebellions were short-lived but had serious repercussions. They often resulted in further persecution, as well as death, for hundreds of thousands of Kurds. Kurdish independence fighters, or **peshmerga** ("those who face death"), and civilians suffered dearly from decades of fighting to achieve an unfulfilled dream. It was not until 1992 that the Kurds of Iraq finally managed to create a form of self-rule, although as a government that was still part of the nation of Iraq.

In Turkey, Kurds make up about 18 percent of the population; in Syria, they make up less than 10 percent; and in Iran, 10 percent. The governments of these three countries raised concerns about the new Iraqi Kurdistan. They viewed the establishment of a separate Kurdish administration in Iraq as a threat to their own stability, because an independent Kurdish state could inspire their minority Kurdish populations to rebel.

It is true that for a century, the Kurds' desire for self-rule has led to instability and violence in the Middle East region. But the Kurds have been fighting for freedoms they have been denied for decades. Some do not see the need for the establishment of a separate Kurdish nation, but simply want the right to practice their own traditions and culture where they live.

After living for a quarter of a century within their **autonomous** government, Iraqi Kurds, who make up 15 to 20 percent of Iraq's population, continue to seek political and cultural rights. This issue became volatile following the second Persian Gulf War in 2003, as the future of the nation of Iraq remained uncertain. Today, Kurds hold top federal posts, and Iraqi Kurdistan (also called the Kurdish Regional Government or KRG) officially operates as an autonomous governing body allied with the central government. Iraqi Kurdistan maintains its own parliament and a military force over which Iraq's Defense Ministry has limited influence. However, Kurdish autonomy is still a volatile issue, especially over whether areas such as Kirkuk—a region with significant oil reserves—should become part of Iraqi Kurdistan.

In present-day Iraq, the Kurdish autonomous region is largely stable and prosperous. However, this stability is threatened by the terrorist group Islamic State of Iraq and the Levant (ISIL), which is attempting to seize control of the Middle East. ISIL is based in Syria and by mid-2015 controlled much of that country. The group has also captured territory in Iraq and Iran and has a small presence in Turkey. In Iraq, the pershmerga have resolutely defended the borders of the autonomous region and protected other areas with large Kurdish populations. The *peshmerga*'s success has reignited nationalist hopes, even though many obstacles to the Kurdish dream of independence remain.

 ## Text-Dependent Questions

1. In what four nations is Kurdistan located?
2. Describe the events that led up to the creation of Iraqi Kurdistan.

 ## Research Project

Use the Internet or a library to research how national boundaries were established in the Kurdistan area after World War I. What reasons were given for the divisions? Was there a movement for the establishment of an independent Kurdish nation at the time? If so, what caused this movement to fail?

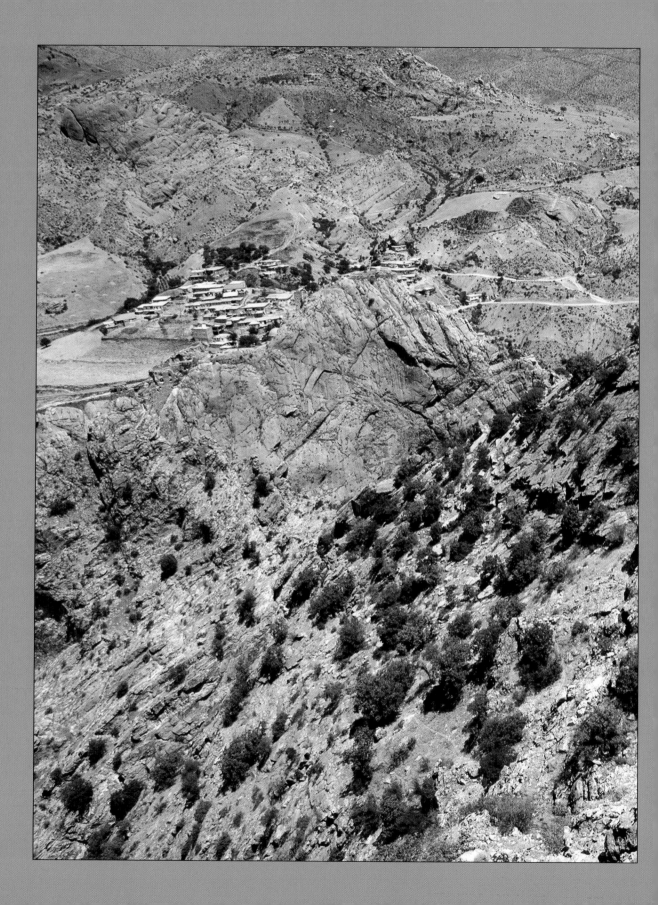

An isolated Kurdish village in the mountains of eastern Turkey. About one-half of Kurdistan, in terms of population and size, can be found within the borders of Turkey.

The Land

Because Kurdistan is not recognized by the rest of the world as an independent nation, its geographical boundaries have never been officially defined. Mapmakers usually indicate the area as the lands containing a majority Kurdish population.

The region known as Kurdistan encompasses parts of eastern Turkey, northeastern Iraq, northwestern Iran, and small portions of Syria, as well as parts of the former Soviet Union. The vast tract is shaped somewhat like a wide-angled upside-down V, with the point of the letter directed toward the Caucasus Mountains of Armenia and Georgia. One arm of the V reaches southwest toward the Mediterranean Sea; the other stretches southeast toward the Persian Gulf.

Estimates of Kurdistan's size vary from as small as 74,000 square miles (191,660 sq km, or about the size of the state of Washington) to as large as 230,000 square miles (595,700 sq km, or slightly smaller than Texas).

LAND OF MOUNTAINS

Kurdistan contains numerous rugged mountains, deep-cut river gorges, sheer rock cliffs, and high plateaus. Its major mountain ranges include the central and northern Zagros of Iran and Iraq, the Elburz (also called Alborz) of Iran, and the eastern third of the Taurus and Pontus of Turkey.

The Zagros mountain system dominates the southeastern part of Kurdistan. This extremely rugged range runs southeast from northern Iraq along the western border of Iran toward the Persian Gulf. Many of its lofty peaks reach higher than 10,000 feet (3,048 meters) and at such great altitudes remain snowcapped year-round. The tallest peak of the Zagros range, called Zard Kuh (or Zardeh Kuh), rises 14,921 feet (4,548 meters) above sea level.

Also in southeastern Kurdistan are the Elburz Mountains, which extend for almost 620 miles (998 km) along the northern border of Iran, just south of the Caspian Sea. In the center of these jagged mountains lies their highest peak, as well as the highest point in Iran—Mount Damavand. A dormant volcano, Mount Damavand rises 18,606 feet (5,671 meters) high. The Elburz range stretches into northeastern Kurdistan, where it meets the highlands and plateaus of the eastern half of the Taurus Mountains. Sometimes the mountains in this area are referred to as the Ararat Mountains. Here, near the border with Armenia and Iran, sits the

Words to Understand in This Chapter

arable—suitable for farming.
steppes—level, treeless, grassy plains that receive little rainfall.

extinct volcano that is Turkey's highest peak. Mount Ararat, thought by some biblical scholars to be the resting place of Noah's ark after the Great Flood, stands 16,949 feet (5,166 meters) high.

Did You Know?

The richest farmland of the Middle East lies within Kurdistan. This productive agricultural region extends from the eastern shore of the Mediterranean Sea, through the Zagros mountain range of Iran and Iraq, to the Persian Gulf.

In western Kurdistan the mountains give way to the lower elevations and rolling hills of Turkey's eastern Anatolian Plateau, which average 1,640 feet (500 meters) above sea level. Toward the south, in the direction of Syria, the mountains descend to the dry *steppes* and flat plains of northern Mesopotamia.

Mesopotamia refers to the ancient region said to be the site of the first human civilization. The word *Mesopotamia* is of Greek origin, and means "land between the rivers." Mesopotamia is embraced by two major rivers of the Middle East—the Tigris (*Dicle*, in Kurdish) and Euphrates. These two rivers, both important sources of irrigation for Syria, Turkey, and Iraq, originate in Kurdistan and flow southeast until they meet in southeastern Iraq and empty into the Persian Gulf.

The northern plains of Mesopotamia include a fertile region known as al-Jazirah, which is Arabic for "the island." For many centuries al-Jazirah served as a huge grazing ground used by the flocks of both Arab and Kurdish nomads. Later it was settled by many Kurds, who farmed the land and helped make it become a major agricultural region, or "breadbasket," of the Middle East.

AN ABUNDANCE OF WATER

Unlike much of the rest of the Middle East, which has little rainfall, Kurdistan can boast of an abundance of water. Numerous rivers rush through the valleys and gorges of the region. Some, such as the Khabur, Tharthar, Ceyhan, Araks, and Kura, have their headwaters in Kurdistan's mountains, but flow mostly outside of Kurdistan's borders. Other rivers flow mainly within Kurdistan, and are a part of the history, culture, and folklore of the Kurds. Among these significant waterways are the Mura and Buhtan Rivers of northern and western Kurdistan (Turkey); the Peshkhabur, the Lesser Zab, the Greater Zab, and the Diyala in central Kurdistan (Iraq); and the Jaghatu, the Tata'u, the Zohab, and the Gamasiyab in southern Kurdistan (Iran).

Besides supplying water for crop irrigation, Kurdistan's rivers have also been harnessed for hydroelectric projects and other industrial uses. The nations of Turkey and Iraq have built huge dams and irrigation projects along the rivers of Kurdistan, often with little concern for the economic consequences that the Kurds living in the region face. Historically, Kurds have had no control over the development of such projects and often have reaped little benefit from them. Fearing a negative impact on the environment and concerned about the flooding of mountain valleys, villages, and ancient historical sites, Kurds as well as other groups have protested dam constructions along Kurdistan's rivers.

One of the most aggressive and controversial dam projects is being built by Turkey. Called the Southeast Anatolia Development Project, or GAP, this $32-billion development plan involves the construction of 22 dams and 19 hydroelectric plants on the Tigris and Euphrates Rivers. Proponents assert that GAP will provide irrigation of arid lands in southeastern Anatolia that will enable millions of Kurdish residents to make a better living. GAP opponents believe the overall venture threatens to destroy the way of life for many Kurds. For example, construction of the Ilisu Dam has already flooded several town and villages, displacing the residents. Some estimates put the total flooded Kurdish villages at 100. Furthermore, the project plans to destroy the archaeological site of

The abandoned Kurdish village of Belkis sits below the Birecik dam on the Euphrates River. The dam, built as part of the Southeast Anatolia Project, will flood numerous villages and archaeological sites. It is estimated that approximately 70,000 Kurds will be displaced by the time the project is complete.

Hasankeyf, an ancient city that dates back at least 5,000 years. When completed, the Southeast Anatolia Development Project will displace more than 70,000 Kurds. Syria and Iraq have protested the GAP because it will reduce the water they receive from the Tigris and Euphrates Rivers.

The inhabitants of Kurdistan cannot look to the region's largest lakes for drinkable water, as the two largest bodies of water are quite salty. In northwest Iran lies the largest salt lake in the Middle East, a shallow body of water known as Lake Urmia. It covers 1,815 square miles (4,701 sq km), reaching a length of about 90 miles (140 km) and a width of 50 miles (80 km), though its deepest depth is just 49 feet (15 meters). The Middle East's second-largest salt

Quick Facts: The Geography of Kurdistan

Location: Middle East and Southwestern Asia, consisting of parts of eastern Turkey, northeastern Iraq, northwestern Iran, and small portions of Syria, Armenia, Azerbaijan, Turkmenistan, and Kazakhstan.

Area: (at largest estimate, slightly smaller than Texas) 230,000 square miles (595,700 sq km).

Unofficial borders: Turkey, Syria, Iraq, Iran, Armenia, Azerbaijan, Georgia, Turkmenistan, and Kazakhstan.

Climate: harsh winters with heavy precipitation; dry summers range from hot to temperate, depending on the elevation.

Terrain: Mostly mountain ranges and plateaus.

Elevation extremes:
> lowest point: Kifri (town in northern Iraq), 544 feet (166 meters) above sea level.
> highest point: Mount Damavand, 18,606 feet (5,671 meters), in Iran.

Natural hazards: periodic droughts in southern Kurdistan, earthquakes.

Source: CIA World Factbook 2015.

lake is Lake Van, located in eastern Turkey near the border with Iran. Lake Van covers 1,434 square miles (3,713 sq km) and reaches more than 74 miles (119 km) at its widest point.

A FERTILE LAND

Many people live in the river valleys, foothills, and rolling plains of Kurdistan, where the abundance of water from rivers, tributaries, and springs has combined with deep, fertile soil to support a variety of crops. About 28 percent of Kurdistan is ***arable***, or suitable for cultivation. Farmers grow wheat and other grains, maintain orchards and vineyards, and raise livestock along the northern slopes of the Elburz Mountains, in the Mus Valley basin (west of Lake Van), and in the wide valleys of northern and central parts of the Zagros Mountains. Areas that do not support crops, such as the higher mountain regions, provide rich pastureland for the grazing of sheep and goats.

CLIMATE EXTREMES

Kurdistan's climate ranges from the extremes of hot, dry summers to severe, bitterly cold winters. At high altitudes heavy snowfalls can occur for a period of up to six months, leaving mountain villages isolated from December to February. Temperatures can fall as low as –20° Fahrenheit (–7° Celsius) in the winter. At the lower elevations of the river valleys, the winter climate is somewhat milder, although it can still be bitterly cold in the lower altitudes of Turkey's Anatolian plateau.

During the summer months, the daytime temperatures become hotter at low elevations than they are in the mountains. At low altitudes, summer temperatures can easily reach above 100°F (38°C), while averaging a mild 68°F (20°C) higher up. In Diyarbakir, the largest Kurdish city in Turkey, the average temperature is 86°F (30°C) in August and 23°F (–5°C) in January.

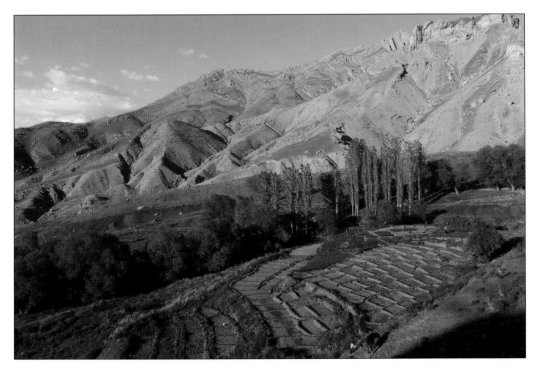

A small Kurdish farm near Dogubeyazit on the Turkey-Iran border.

Kurdistan's many rivers are fed by large amounts of precipitation, much of which falls as snow between November and April, and then melts in the spring. Precipitation is greatest in central Kurdistan, which averages about 60 to 80 inches (150 to 200 cm) per year. The lower elevations of western Kurdistan, where steppes dominate, receive much less precipitation, averaging 20 to 40 inches (50 to 102 cm) per year. In the Kurdish region of Iraq, dry summers are often accompanied by a hot, dusty northwesterly wind called the shamal. This area also suffers from periodic droughts.

FLORA AND FAUNA

A hundred years ago, large stands of ancient oak forests covered much of Kurdistan. However, few large trees remain today. Over the years, much of the region's forest cover was cut down to build houses or for firewood. Within the past few decades many large trees were destroyed by warfare. This has sometimes been done purposely by the governments of Turkey, Iran, Iraq, and Syria, so the forests would not provide cover for Kurdish *peshmerga* fighters.

Today, twisted scrub oaks make up much of the remaining forestland in Kurdistan, although some forests may also contain cedars, chestnuts, junipers, poplars, pines, and wild fruit trees. In some wooded areas, Kurds harvest crops that have sprung up in the wild, such as fruits (grapes, cherries, and pears), berries (mulberries and blackberries), and nuts (hazelnuts, walnuts, chestnuts, and almonds).

Wildflowers are perhaps the best-known flora of Kurdistan. Flowers like the white *nergiz* (narcissus); purple, yellow, and red *sheqayiq* (ranunculus); and red *gulale* (poppy) blanket the mountainsides in the springtime and early summer. In ancient times the sheep and goats feeding on these sweet-smelling flowers produced delicious milk. According to legend, the butter made from this milk brought Vikings all the way from Scandinavia to buy it.

The forests and rivers also provide ample nourishment for the fauna of Kurdistan, which include wild black and brown bears, boars, beavers, cheetahs, hyenas, leopards, and wolves. Fish such as carp and trout abound in the region's freshwater lakes and rivers. Among Kurdistan's many native birds are bluebirds, eagles, larks, quail, and partridges. Some Kurdish families keep the *kau*, a gray bird of the partridge family, as a pet so they can enjoy its melodic song.

EARTHQUAKES

Kurdistan sees frequent earthquake activity, as it is located within the Alpide seismic belt, an area that has seen some of the world's most destructive earthquakes. Kurdish folk tales and legends tell of entire villages being swallowed up. Considering just how unstable the earth in this region is, it is possible these stories are largely true. Lava flows have created natural dams that have blocked river channels, forming vast lakes such as Urmia and Van.

 # Text-Dependent Questions

1. Describe the landscape of Kurdistan.
2. What two major rivers originate in Kurdistan?
3. Name five wild animals that live in Kurdistan.

 # Research Project

Use the Internet to locate estimates of the size and unofficial boundaries of Kurdistan. Make a table of the data you find. Create columns for the source (organization or government) that provided the information, the total estimated area, and a description of the estimated borders. In a notes column, hypothesize whether the source may have a reason to overestimate or underestimate the data, or if the source may include or exclude a specific region because of their own interests (political, religious, etc.).

An armed guard stands on the roof of a Baghdad office building belonging to the Patriotic Union of Kurdistan (PUK). In Iraq, two groups have fought for supremacy in Iraqi Kurdistan, the PUK and the rival Kurdistan Democratic Party (KDP). They currently share power, but divisions between the parties remain.

History

An ancient people, the Kurds are thought to have descended from Indo-European tribes of central Asia that moved westwards across Iran around 1500 BCE. Eventually, these groups made the Zagros and Taurus Mountains their homeland. Written records dating from the seventh century BCE contain the first mention of Kurdish people, indicating they lived in the southern region of Lake Van, in present-day Turkey. The Greek general and historian Xenophon, who lived around 400 BCE, also described a people who most likely were Kurds. According to his writings, the Karduchoi, as they were called, were fierce fighters.

Although the mountainous lands where they lived changed hands many times as empires rose and fell (among the rulers were the Sumerians, Akkadians, Babylonians, Assyrians, Parthians, Persians, Romans, and Armenians), the Kurds did not change much in their way of life. They considered their tribal leaders the ultimate authority, not the imperial government that ruled them.

Self-governing Kurdish tribal communities would pay tribute to the ruling regime, but the independent-minded Kurds mostly maintained their nomadic lifestyle as they tended their flocks and herds.

ISLAMIC EMPIRES

While many things remained the same for the Kurds under foreign powers, their religious faith did not. During the seventh century CE Arab peoples gained control of Kurdistan and brought with them a new religion known as Islam. Founded by the prophet Muhammad, who was born around 570 CE, Islam holds that there is only one God, called Allah. Muslims—followers of the Islamic faith—believe that the word of Allah was revealed to Muhammad, who then taught it to his followers. Later, those teachings were collected into the **Qur'an**, the holy book of Islam.

Upon Muhammad's death in 632, the Muslim community split into two factions. One group, the **Shiites**, believed that Muhammad's son-in-law Ali was the prophet's heir and the rightful leader of Islam. The

Words to Understand in This Chapter

caliph—title for the religious and political leader of Muslims. In the Ottoman empire, the sultan claimed this position, but after the breakup of the empire the caliphate was abolished.

crusade—any war or campaign that is religiously motivated; the Crusades were military campaigns carried out by European Christians between the 11th and 13th centuries to take the Holy Land of Jerusalem from Muslim control.

mandate—authority given by the League of Nations that its member nations administer and establish a government over territories taken from defeated empires after World War I.

martial law—the law applied in an occupied territory by military authority.

Qur'an—the sacred book of Muslims, believed to be the word of Allah dictated to the prophet Muhammad by the angel Gabriel.

shah—a king or sovereign ruler of Persia or Iran.

Shiites—followers of the main minority sect of Islam; they believe the descendants of Ali (Muhammad's son-in-law) to be rightful heirs of the prophet Muhammad.

sultan—ruler of the Ottoman Empire.

name of this religious group comes from the Arabic phrase *shiat Ali*, which means "the party of Ali." A second group, the Sunnis, believed that the spiritual and political rulers of the Islamic state, or **caliphs**, should be chosen by consensus. The name *Sunni* derives from the Arabic word Sunna, which means "tradition." Sunni Muslims believe they are the true followers of the traditions of Muhammad and his community. They grew to become the dominant faction of Islam.

During the 600s, Islam spread quickly as Muslim Arabs conquered the lands of modern-day Egypt, Syria, and Iraq. By 711 CE Arab Islamic empires reached from present-day Spain to Iran. As the lands of the Kurds came under Islamic rule, most Kurdish people converted to the Sunni Muslim faith. However, they did not adopt the Arabic language.

The Muslim conqueror Salah ad-Din (known in the West as Saladin) accepts the surrender of Jerusalem in 1187 by the descendants of European Crusaders who had captured the city nearly a century earlier. Most Muslims consider Salah ad-Din a hero, but he is particularly revered by Kurds.

Over the centuries many Kurdish tribes formed military groups that fought for various Islamic empires. Most Kurds today take special pride in their famous ancestor Salah ad-Din Yusuf ibn Ayyub, known to the Western world as Saladin. He was a Kurdish military leader who in the late 12th century united the Muslim lands of Syria, northern Mesopotamia (Iraq), Kurdistan, Palestine, and Egypt. In 1187, he led a Muslim army that recaptured Jerusalem and other cities from European Christians, who had conquered the region during the First **Crusade** in 1096–99. To many Kurds, Saladin is a national hero and a renowned champion of Islam, celebrated for liberating Muslim lands from the Europeans.

Although descendants of Saladin ruled his Ayyubid Empire for several generations, the empire soon fell and the Mongols from Central Asia took control of Kurdish lands. The region was important, because Kurdistan was a part of the Silk Road, a series of trade routes that linked Asia with Europe. Merchants and traders traveling the Silk Road also purchased Kurdish handicrafts, particularly the region's famous woven rugs.

THE OTTOMAN EMPIRE

The 14th century saw the rise of the Ottoman empire, named for its first **sultan**, Osman I. During the 1300s and 1400s Ottoman forces swept across the Anatolian plateau. In 1453, they captured the city of Constantinople, bringing to an end the powerful Byzantine empire. The Ottomans renamed the city Istanbul and made it their capital. The Ottoman empire became the strongest power in the region, conquering and controlling vast territories. At its peak in the 16th and 17th centuries, the kingdom included not only Kurdistan and Mesopotamia but also lands in present-day northern Africa and southeastern Europe.

For centuries, the majority of Kurds lived under the rule of the Ottoman sultans, although some Kurdish people were governed by

After conquering Constantinople in 1453, the Ottoman Empire continued to expand its boundaries during the 15th and 16th centuries. The empire reached its height in 1672, when it controlled much of the Middle East as well as large parts of north Africa, central Asia, and eastern Europe. Although the empire had lost much of its territory by the start of World War I (1914) it still included most of Kurdistan. After the war, the modern state of Turkey was established by the Treaty of Lausanne (1923), and control over Kurdistan and other former Ottoman territories was divided among the victorious allied powers.

Persian **shahs** of the Safavid empire (1501–1722). This empire, which was ruled by Shiite Muslims, controlled lands east of the Ottoman empire, including the area of modern-day Iran.

In both the Ottoman and the Safavid empires, Kurdish princes governed tribal communities, or emirates. Sultans and shahs gave the princes semi-autonomous powers in return for paying tribute or providing Kurdish fighters to the empire. In the Kurdish areas within the Ottoman empire (particularly present-day Iraq and Turkey) there were 16 large emirates and approximately 50 Kurdish fief-doms, or smaller kingdoms. The courts in these principalities featured much learning, with poets, scientists, and religious scholars held in high esteem.

During the 19th century, some Kurdish princes began to fight against the Ottoman empire for independence. At the same time, the empire was weakening just as several European nations were growing stronger. In 1914, Sultan Muhammad VI brought the Ottoman empire into World War I on the side of Germany and against the alliance of France, Italy, Russia, and the United Kingdom. After Germany's defeat in 1918, the victorious Allies divided the lands of the Ottoman empire. The Kurdish people awaited the partitioning eagerly, for they had been promised that the region known as Kurdistan would officially be made a separate nation.

PROMISE OF INDEPENDENCE

The Treaty of Sevres, signed in 1920 by the Ottoman sultan and representatives of the triumphant European countries, called for the establishment of a Kurdish state. However, that independent nation was never realized.

Although the Ottoman sultan had surrendered, one of his generals would not. Mustafa Kemal (more popularly known as Mustafa Atatürk, the name he later took as president) refused to submit to the demands of the Treaty of Sevres, and his Turkish military forces continued fighting. Their victories forced the Allies to renegotiate the Sevres peace treaty, which in 1923 was replaced by the Treaty of Lausanne. The latter agreement

 Did You Know?

Tikrit, Iraq, is the birthplace of one of the Kurds' most beloved political figures, the 12th-century military leader Saladin. It is also the birthplace of one of their most hated: Iraqi dictator Saddam Hussein, who before his removal in April 2003 was responsible for the deaths of hundreds of thousands of Kurds.

created the independent nation that the Turkish general wanted. Called the Republic of Turkey, the newly created country had boundaries that cut deeply into northern Kurdistan.

The League of Nations, an international organization created after World War I to promote worldwide peace and security, authorized France and Britain to rule newly created Middle East territories as **mandates**. France received a mandate to rule Syria, which included part of southern Kurdistan. Great Britain controlled Mesopotamia, renamed Iraq, which was created from the Ottoman *vilayets*, or provinces, of Baghdad, Basra, and Mosul. (The Kurds still consider the oil-rich Mosul region part of southern Kurdistan.)

As a result of the Treaty of Lausanne, the Kurdish people had become minority groups in three different nations: Turkey, Iraq, and Syria. Those living in Persia had been a minority since the 1500s.

A MINORITY IN TURKEY

Following its official creation in 1923, Turkey worked to impose unity on the population within its boundaries. The country refused to acknowledge that separate ethnic groups even existed. Everyone was a Turk according to President Atatürk (whose name, which means "the father of all Turks," reflected his unifying mission). Subsequently, the Kurds were deemed "mountain Turks" who had forgotten their language.

The government refused to recognize Kurdish linguistic or cultural rights. Turkish laws prohibited Kurds from speaking their native language in public, teaching or publishing in the Kurdish language, or using Kurdish in the courts or government offices. Even the word *Kurdistan* was removed from official documents. The new Turkish state established a centralized taxation system on Kurdish lands, effectively taking away the Kurds' financial autonomy. Atatürk abolished the Muslim caliphate as well, an action that angered many religious Kurds.

A painting of Mustafa Kemal Atatürk (1881–1938), the founder of modern Turkey. As president of Turkey, Atatürk refused to officially admit that the Kurds were a separate ethnic group, and Kurds lost their cultural and economic rights in the new state.

As their cultural, economic, and religious rights were taken away, the Kurds revolted in 1925 under the leadership of Sheikh Said Piran. His forces were quickly crushed. Subsequent uprisings during the 1930s were similarly put down, as thousands of Kurds were killed and as many as a million lost their homes to bombings.

In the decades that followed, few Kurds made an attempt to revive a Kurdish nationalist movement. It was not until 1978 that student activist Abdullah Öcalan founded the Kurdish Workers' Party (Partiya Karkere Kurdistan, or PKK). The party advocated for a completely independent Kurdish state, and sought this goal by any means possible. In 1984, open warfare broke out between Turkish government forces and the PKK in various parts of southeastern Turkey. As leader of the PKK, Öcalan directed the attacks and battle operations from his base in Syria.

Soon the PKK engaged in violence not only against Turkish troops, but against anyone identified as a government collaborator. Targets included schoolteachers (for forcing the Turkish language upon Kurds) and government workers such as police officers, state officials, and village guards. The PKK struck not only in southeastern Turkey but also in its western cities and in other European nations. Although several countries, including Turkey and the United States, identified the PKK as a terrorist organization, it continued to find a large following among Kurdish residents of Turkey who resented the Turkish government's oppression.

The Turkish government responded to the PKK attacks by establishing state-of-emergency rule, or ***martial law***, in southeastern Turkey and bringing in approximately 220,000 Turkish troops. Many Kurds suffered under emergency rule, which permitted authorities to hold suspects in confinement for 30 days, as well as deny them the right to an appeal. In 1992, convinced that the Kurds living in the southeastern region were sympathetic to the PKK rebels, Turkish government forces emptied and burned thousands of villages, many along the border with Iraq. Military troops, gunships, and helicopters forcibly evicted Kurds from their mountain farmlands. An estimated 3 million refugees fled to the Kurdish city of Diyarbakir and even further to the western Turkish cities of Ankara and Istanbul.

During the early 1990s, Turkish President Turgut Özal urged the government to address the Kurdish issue. Eager to institute

Kurds in Istanbul protest the killing of three female members of the PKK in 2012.

reforms, Özal acknowledged that Kurds were a separate ethnic group. He promoted changes in the laws to permit Kurdish song, speech, and music, although the use of Kurdish in the courts, in schools, and in radio and television broadcasts remained prohibited. However, his sudden death in 1993 from a heart attack hindered further progress in granting Kurdish rights.

PKK rebels operated from bases in Syria and Iraq, just across the border, so they could strike in rural southeastern Turkey and then retreat to safety. Turkish troops occasionally crossed the border into northern Iraq to attack PKK bases there.

The years of warfare took a severe toll on the Kurds of Turkey. During that time, human rights organizations documented assassinations, disappearances, firebombing of homes, and torture by police. Human Rights Watch estimated that more than 3,000

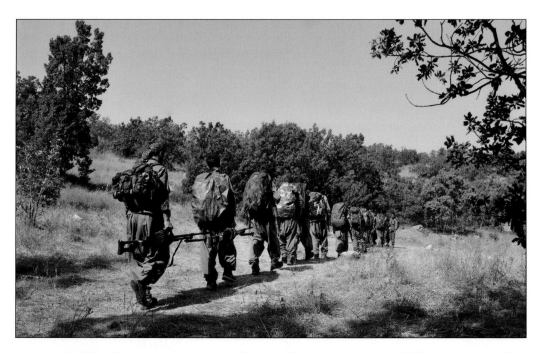

A group of PKK militants on the move in the Qandil Mountains of Iraq, 2013. The organization once used this region to launch attacks against Turkey, but it declared a cease-fire in 2013. During 2014 and 2015, PKK soldiers joined the *peshmerga* in Iraqi Kurdistan in military operations against ISIL forces.

Kurdish villages in Turkey were destroyed between 1984 and 1994, and more than 250,000 Kurds were made homeless. More than 30,000 people—military personnel and civilians—lost their lives as a result of the conflicts between the PKK and Turkish government.

Turkey's government captured Öcalan in 1999 (he is now serving a life sentence), and soon after, the PKK agreed to a ceasefire. In 2002, the PKK renamed itself the Kurdish Congress for Freedom and Democracy, or KADEK, and announced that it now favored increased Kurdish autonomy and rights within Turkey. However, the ceasefire broke down in 2003. Many observers suggested that the best way for Turkey to halt the spread of the PKK would be to improve its treatment of the Kurds.

Under pressure from the European Union, Turkish legislators made some recent changes to benefit the Kurdish population. New laws ended bans on teaching Kurdish and giving children Kurdish names. They also allowed for state television and radio stations to broadcast in Kurdish. Around the same time the state of emergency in most of southeastern Turkey was lifted, and many rural Kurds were allowed to return to their villages. In 2008, to create jobs, Turkey's government announced plans for infrastructure projects in the Kurdish southeast, including road repair and dam construction.

PKK and Turkish leaders occasionally met for talks, but little progress resulted until recently. From his prison cell, Öcalan called for the Kurdish militants to put down their arms in 2013. In 2015, the Turkish government announced an agreement for a complete disarmament.

A MINORITY IN IRAQ

The Kurds of Iraq rebelled first against the British mandate and later against the constitutional monarchy of Emir Faisal, whom the British placed on the throne in 1932 and continued to support militarily. In 1919, 1922, and 1923 Sheikh Mahmoud Barzinji led several unsuccessful Kurdish uprisings. They were followed in 1932 by a rebellion led by Mulla Mustafa Barzani and his older brother, Ahmad. Although Mustafa's uprising was also crushed, the Kurdish leader would persist for 40 more years as he waged campaigns for a separate Kurdish state and earned the appreciation and love of his people.

In 1943 Barzani's Kurdish forces captured regions around the cities of Erbil and Badinan, but British warplanes pushed his *peshmerga* militia out of Iraq and into Iran. There Barzani's forces joined with rebellious Iranian Kurds and in 1946 declared an independent Kurdish state called the Mahabad Republic. Supported by the Soviet Union and administered by the newly established Kurdistan Democratic Party (KDP), the Mahabad Republic lasted for less than a year and then collapsed. Barzani, who had served as commander-in-chief of the short-lived government, fled to the Soviet Union.

During the next decade, the KDP regained strength in Iraq. In July 1958, the Iraqi monarchy was overthrown by a group of military officers led by General Abd al-Karim Qasim. Believing that the coup signaled positive change, Mulla Mustafa returned from exile. The future looked promising: a new Iraqi constitution promised national rights for Kurds, now considered a part of the new Iraqi state; they were allowed to broadcast and publish in Kurdish; and they could attend Kurdish schools ranging from the elementary to the university level.

However, although Iraq was called a republic it was effectively run by a series of dictators who rejected the idea of granting autonomy to the Kurds. By 1961 the KDP had been banned, and Kurds under the leadership of Mulla Mustafa were battling the government. Fighting did not end until March 1970, when the Kurds were granted rights in a peace accord signed by Barzani and Saddam Hussein, then the vice president of the Baath Party, which had come into power in 1968.

In March 1974, Iraqi president Ahmed Hasan al-Bakr released an official proclamation defining Iraqi Kurdistan as an autonomous province within Iraq, with Erbil as its capital. The announcement established an elected legislative assembly and executive council, and identified Kurdish as one of Iraq's official languages. However, the plan had several points that the Kurds disputed. Barzani, who had become leader of the Kurdistan Democratic Party, rejected the proposal because it failed to include half of what the Kurds considered their land, including the oil-rich region around the city of Kirkuk. It also did not provide an adequate share of oil revenues, or allow for fair Kurdish representation in the Iraqi government.

Kurdish leaders Massoud Barzani (right) of the KDP and Jalal Talabani of the PUK stand together in front of a painting of Mustafa Barzani, the father of Kurdish nationalism in Iraq.

Civil war resumed in March 1974, with Iran, Israel, and the United States providing the Kurds with much-needed support. However, a year later these countries withdrew their backing. The Kurdish uprising in Iraq collapsed, and, fearing a severe reprisal by the Iraqi Baathist government, more than 100,000 Kurds fled to Iran. Thousands who remained were killed by Iraqi forces. Barzani fled to the United States, where he died in 1979.

Dissent within the KDP resulted in the creation of a new political party. In 1975 former KDP member Jalal Talabani founded the Patriotic Union of Kurdistan (PUK). The group soon clashed with the KDP, led by Mustafa's son, Massoud Barzani.

Meanwhile, the ruling Baath party began instituting policies to acquire greater control of the oil in Kurdish territory. In the mid-1970s the government implemented the policy of "Arabization" of oil-rich Kurdish areas, particularly in Kirkuk and Khanaqin. To transform the populations in these regions from predominantly Kurdish to Arab, government troops evicted Kurdish farmers and replaced them with Arab tribesmen. More than half of Iraq's Kurds were displaced. Around the same time the government forbid any teaching in Kurdish and closed Kurdish schools and universities.

In 1979 al-Bakr resigned the Iraqi presidency, and the Baathist regime continued under Saddam Hussein, who ruled as dictator. One of his first major actions as president was to invade Iraq's long-time enemy, Iran, in 1980. The Kurds became embroiled in the ensuing eight-year-long conflict, as both countries contended for Kurdish territory in northern Iraq. The Kurds sided with Iran against the Baghdad government, and they paid dearly for their allegiance. In 1983 all Iraqi Kurdish villages within 12.5 miles (20 km) of the Iranian border were destroyed as Saddam Hussein's forces moved their inhabitants into "collective towns," located in army-controlled areas of northern Iraq. Some Kurds were relocated to barren desert towns in southern Iraq, while thousands of male Kurds over the age of 12 simply disappeared. It was later learned that they had been rounded up, executed, and buried in mass graves.

The lack of international outcry over this massacre led to further atrocities. In 1988, from February 23 until September 6, the Iraqi Anfal military campaign led by Ali Hassan al-Majid killed thousands of Kurds. Later nicknamed "Chemical Ali," al-Majid had clearance to use chemical weapons to kill thousands of Kurdish men, women, and children. His goal, in his own words, was "to solve the Kurdish problem and slaughter the saboteurs." To accomplish this, his men systematically destroyed approximately 1,200

Kurdish villages by bulldozing the buildings, covering wells and springs with concrete, and poisoning the fields.

In the village of Halabja alone, approximately 6,000 Kurds were massacred by poison gas dropped by Iraqi government bombs in 1988. Thousands more Kurds were rounded up and sent to refugee camps, where they received no food, water, or shelter (they survived only because of secret help from nearby residents). As many as 180,000 men were executed and their bodies bulldozed into mass graves.

In August 1990, Iraq invaded its neighbor to the south, Kuwait. In response, a coalition of 34 nations, including the United States, went to war against the Iraqi government of Saddam Hussein. Begun in mid-January 1991, the first Persian Gulf War ended at the end of February with the expulsion of Iraqi forces from Kuwait.

Iraqi president Saddam Hussein, holding a rifle, observes a military parade with General Ali Hassan al-Majid. Known to Kurds as "Chemical Ali," the general was responsible for attacks on Kurdish civilians, including the massacre at Halabja. Both were captured following the second Gulf War, and faced trial for their crimes. Both were found guilty. Saddam was executed in 2006, Hassan al-Majid in 2010.

Soon after, in March 1991, the Kurds once again rose up against the Iraqi government. However, the *peshmerga* forces received little support from the allied coalition, and were soon crushed by Saddam Hussein's army, the Republican Guard. More than a million Kurdish refugees fled to the borders of Turkey and Iran, but, fearing refugee camps within its borders might foster the Kurdish nationalist movement, Turkey prevented many from entering. About 500,000 Kurdish refugees

U.S. soldiers carry Kurdish children into a refugee camp, May 1991. When Saddam Hussein attacked Iraq's Kurdish population after losing the Gulf War, hundreds of thousands of Kurds fled from their homes into refugee camps in the mountains along the borders with Turkey and Iran.

were forced to remain in northern Iraq, living in makeshift camps in the mountains.

With little food and shelter, thousands of Kurds died. But this time the world was paying attention. As television and newspaper reports told of their plight, some members of the Gulf War coalition took action. France, Great Britain, and the United States established Operation Provide Comfort, an American-led program to provide food and shelter for refugees. The coalition nations also agreed to establish airspace over northern Iraq where Iraqi planes were forbidden to fly. Kurds living in this "no-fly zone," located north of the 36th parallel of latitude, would be protected from future bombing attacks by the Iraqi government.

Within this protected zone, Iraqi Kurds took charge, administering the region as the newly created Kurdish Regional Government (KRG). But although Jalal Talabani's PUK and Massoud Barzani's KDP had united in 1991 to fight against Saddam Hussein, they clashed as rival leaders of the autonomous region. In 1994, an internal war began. Two years into the conflict, the KDP even formed an alliance with Saddam Hussein to fight against the PUK, which was receiving military assistance from Iran. Iraqi troops and tanks initially helped the KDP defeat its opponents, but the United States stepped in to prevent Saddam from interfering in the region, extending the no-fly zone to within 30 miles (48 km) of Baghdad and striking against Iraqi missile sites in the south.

Bloody warfare between the two major Iraqi Kurdish parties lasted until 1998, when their leaders agreed to officially divide the region between them and signed a peace accord brokered by the United States. But their four-year conflict had caused thousands of deaths and displaced tens of thousands more.

Through the years Saddam continued with his policy of Arabization in Kurdish regions outside the protected zone. In the region of Kirkuk alone, approximately 250,000 Kurds were deported. Those who remained were barred from owning property and registering businesses or marriages unless they assumed Arabic names and changed their ethnicity to "Arab" on official documents. Street names and districts received new Arabic names, and Arabs continued to be offered financial rewards for settling in the region.

For years, Iraq disregarded orders by the United Nations that it comply with restrictions imposed after the 1991 Persian Gulf War. U.S.-led forces finally attacked the country in March 2003, which began the second Persian Gulf War. A month later, U.S. troops entered Baghdad, which they took with little resistance. During the combat operations, approximately 70,000 Kurdish militia troops placed themselves under U.S. command and helped take control of the oil-rich towns of Kirkuk and Mosul.

On April 9, 2003, Saddam's regime was officially toppled, and the United States set up a Coalition Provisional Authority (CPA) to administer the war-torn nation until a constitution could be written and elections held. Two months later, the Iraqi Governing Council was appointed, which included Kurds among its members. In March 2004 the Iraqi Governing Council approved a preliminary constitution that allowed for Kurdish representation at the highest level of government.

Violent incidents in Iraq continued after war's end; some of these attacks targeted Kurds because of their support for U.S. intervention in the country. The PUK and KDP suffered a horrific terrorist attack in February 2004 when suicide bombers devastated the two main Kurdish party offices in Erbil. The blasts killed more than 100 Kurds, including the Kurdish deputy prime minister and the city's governor and lieutenant governor. Members of Ansar al-Islam, a group of Kurdish religious extremists who had threatened the PUK and KDP in the past, were blamed for the attacks.

Tensions have remained high between the Kurds and other ethnic groups in northern Iraq as questions over land rights, militias, and the future government have occupied all Iraqi citizens. While Kurds sacrifice their lives to keep Kurdish regions out of ISIL control, some Arab Iraqis in the disputed areas around Kirkuk and Mosul support ISIL.

Postwar turmoil and years of devastating violence have threatened the political process in Iraq. Coalition forces and other international groups have supervised a long stabilization process, but the land-grabbing techniques of the Islamic State threaten to topple the shaky central government. As the Iraqi government weakens, Kurdish arguments for independence grow stronger. President Barzani has pledge that the Kurdish Regional Government will soon hold a referendum on independence.

A MINORITY IN IRAN

In 1921, army officer Reza Khan took power over Iran in a military coup, founding the Pahlavi dynasty and assuming the title of shah. Although the Kurds in Iran rose up against him in the 1920s, they failed to break away from his government. From 1925 to 1941, the Kurds lived under the rule of Reza Shah Pahlavi, as he was later called. He was succeeded by his son Mohammad Reza Pahlavi.

About 20 years after their first rebellion, Iranian Kurds were briefly successful in creating their own independent nation. In January 1946, Kurdish leader Qazi Mohamed proclaimed the founding of the Mahabad Republic, a new Kurdish nation located in a sliver of northwestern Iraq and based in the town of Mahabad. Qazi Mohamed, who was supported by Iraqi Kurds and the newly created Kurdistan Democratic Party, assumed the presidency. The fledgling nation was backed by the Soviet Union, but vehemently opposed by the Iranian monarchy, Britain, and the United States. When the Soviets abandoned their support, the Mahabad Republic fell within the year to Iranian forces, and its Kurdish founder was hanged.

Several decades later, in the late 1970s, Kurdish nationalists again tried to break away from Iran. The 1979 Islamic revolution that forced Shah Mohammad Reza Pahlavi from power put the country in turmoil. While conservative clerical forces established a Shiite Islamic government headed by religious leader Ayatollah Ruholla Khomeini, Abdul Rahman Qassemlou led the Kurdish Democratic Party of Iran (KDPI) in a bid to gain control of Kurdish land.

From 1979 to 1982, Kurdish guerrilla fighters battled the Islamic Revolution Guards, the Iranian government's armed forces. The Iran-Iraq War began around the same time, and eventually more than 25,000 Kurdish civilians lost their lives in the crossfire. By 1983, the government of the Islamic Republic had regained control of the Kurdish region. It outlawed the KDPI, and those members who had not escaped to northern Iraq were executed. After the Iran-Iraq War ended in 1988, Abdul Rahman Qassemlou and several other well-known Kurdish leaders were assassinated while meeting in Europe with Iranian authorities.

The Islamic Revolution Guards remained in control of the Kurdish areas of Iran until 1998. At that time, Iran's National Security Council declared the region "secure" and transferred responsibility for maintaining law and order to the local police.

Under the shah of Iran the separate Kurdish identity had been recognized, but the government had forbidden Kurds from publishing Kurdish books or speaking their language in public. Many of those involved in Kurdish politics were jailed. Establishment of the new Islamic Republic brought new restrictions, particularly with its enforcement of Islamic law, or *Sharia*, under which strict religious observances became mandatory. Farsi was declared the official language of all Iran, which effectively prevented Kurds from studying in their own language. Nonetheless, Iranian Kurds eventually gained more freedoms than they had enjoyed under the shah.

Beginning in 1998, Iran's president Mohammad Khatami granted some additional rights to Kurds, allowing them better representation in local governments and opening up cultural opportunities. Some Kurds were elected to Iran's parliament. And with the appropriate government permit in hand, Iranian Kurds could perform traditional plays and music in public. The government also permitted students to learn Kurdish and publishers to produce Kurdish-language newspapers and journals.

However, the Sunni Muslim Kurds are still viewed with suspicion by Iran's Shiite government and Kurdish calls for autonomy are violently answered. Iranian leaders also fear that Iraqi Kurds' political gains could inspire revolt in the heavily Kurdish province of Kordestan. Iran has shelled some Iraqi border towns, claiming Kurdish separatists based there have attacked Iranian targets.

A MINORITY IN SYRIA

The population of Syrian Kurds is estimated below 1.7 million in a country of almost 18 million, or less than 10 percent of Syria's population. Like Kurds of other countries, Syrian Kurds also struggle for basic rights. For nearly 50 years, from 1963 to 2011, they lived under emergency law in the Republic of Syria.

This rare color image, taken by a Russian photographer around 1905, shows a Kurdish woman with her children.

Although the government initially allowed certain cultural and religious freedoms for Kurds, by the 1950s Syrian laws banned the teaching of Kurdish in schools; the publication of Kurdish-language materials; and the formation of Kurdish political parties. In 1961 the government took steps to take lands from Kurds living within the oil-rich al-Jazira region by stripping more than 100,000 of them and their descendants of their citizenship. Two years later, an Arabization resettlement program began forcing many Kurds to move.

By 2010, the number of Kurds in Syria who lacked legal citizenship numbered approximately 300,000. They were denied the right to vote, own property, obtain government jobs, or even get a passport. Finally in 2011, the Syrian government granted citizenship to most of the nation's Kurdish population. However, approximately 80,000 Kurds remain stateless.

The Kurds of Syria are allowed to speak their native tongue, but they cannot legally publish, teach, or write in Kurdish. At times, Kurdish men have been forbidden from wearing their traditional dress, although there have been no such restrictions on women. Kurds cannot form independent political parties, and activists for reform have been jailed, tortured, exiled, and killed.

The Kurds' frustration over their second-class status has seldom

A Syrian army heilcopter flies overhead as more than 20,000 Kurds celebrate the festival of Newroz in Qamlo, Syria, during March 2013.

erupted into violence. However, in March 2004 ethnic unrest between Kurds and Arabs at a soccer game in the multi-ethnic city of Qamishli (Kamishli), located north of Damascus, soon developed into antigovernment protests that spread to other cities across northeastern Syria. Demonstrators waved the Kurdish flag, set fire to government buildings, and defaced images and statues of former president Hafiz al-Assad. Government forces fired on the protesters, killing approximately 30 to 40 of them and wounding several hundred more. In the weeks that followed, Syrian police arrested thousands more in crackdowns in the cities of Damascus and Aleppo.

Government officials blamed the Kurdish unrest in Syria on the gains being made by Kurds in Iraq. In June 2005, Kurdish demonstrations again turned violent, when police clashed with protestors calling for citizenship for the stateless. The unsolved murder of a Kurdish cleric seemed to be the catalyst.

Following the Syrian government's violent opposition to pro-democracy demonstrations in 2011, the nation fell into civil war. Syrian Kurdish militias have found themselves fighting forces of President Assad, Islamist rebels, and the Islamic State who has taken advantage of the civil war to seize large areas of the country. Kurdish focus has been on protecting Kurdish land, rather than on either overthrowing or protecting the Assad regime.

Throughout the conflict, the Kurdish militia has been largely successful in keeping peace in the Kurdish northeastern corner of Syria. In late 2013, the region declared autonomy from the central government, further establishing its separation from any of the factions of the war. Kurdish leaders say they do not want separation from Syria, but a strong local government similar to Iraqi Kurdistan. The region is called Rojava, or Western Kurdistan. Recognizing Syria's Kurdish population as a key ally in the struggle against ISIL, the central government announced it would negotiate the details of an autonomous Kurdish region within Syria in March of 2015.

 ## Text-Dependent Questions

1. What historic city was renamed Istanbul by the Ottomans?
2. Why was the Treaty of Sevres renegotiated?
3. What prevented the establishment of Iraqi Kurdistan in 1974?

 ## Research Project

Use the Internet or a library to research the 12th-century leader Saladin. Write a short biography of Saladin that describes the major events in his life, his accomplishments, and his contributions to the Muslim world.

A Kurdish man prays in a mosque in Erbil, Iraq. Most of the Kurds follow Islam, the dominant religion of the Middle East, although a small minority practice other religions.

The Economy, Politics, and Religion

For centuries Kurds made their living by farming and raising cattle, sheep, and goats; however, with the discovery of oil in the early 20th century and its subsequent development, the means of income have changed for many Kurds.

Centuries ago, farmers from Kurdistan provided much of the region's meat to people living in the surrounding areas of Anatolia, Syria, and Mesopotamia. Today, Kurds still raise livestock for their meat as well as their wool and milk. Sheep and goats are herded to high mountain pastures in the summer, and brought to lowland plains during the winter months. Villagers raise cows and bulls for their meat and milk, and for power in pulling carts and plows. Some Kurds also raise chickens for eggs and meat.

In arable parts of Kurdistan, farmers raise grains (wheat, barley, rye, and oats), as well as crops such as oil seeds (sesame and sunflower), fruits and vegetables (tomatoes, cucumber, watermelon, melon, onion, and garlic, apples, apricots, grapes, olives, peaches, pears, plums, and pomegranates), and legumes (chickpeas, lentils, and green beans). Some fruit and nut trees that grow in the wild in the Zagros and Taurus mountain ranges provide pistachios, almonds, hazelnuts, and chestnuts. The principal cash crops, however, are tobacco and cotton.

In the cities and towns of Turkey, Iraq, Iran, and Syria, many Kurds work as unskilled laborers, particularly in construction. Some do more skilled work as bricklayers, butchers, cattle dealers, and as supervisors or foremen over manual laborers.

Many Kurds have spent their lives as fighters, living for years at a time in the rugged mountains of Kurdistan. In the past, Kurdish tribal chiefs supported *peshmerga* fighters, calling them into service when they were needed. More recently, people living in nearby villages have supported *peshmerga* guerrillas with food and other necessities. In Iraq, the term *peshmerga* is also used to refer to those whom political parties hire as militia fighters.

MANUFACTURING AND ENERGY

Despite the large amount of cotton and wool that Kurdistan produces and the reputation Kurds have for weaving carpets and kilims (richly colored rugs with intricate patterns), the region has no large-scale textile industry. Most cotton and wool is used for local weaving and other Kurdish handicrafts. For the most part, textiles are imported rather than exported.

Words to Understand in This Chapter

embargo—a prohibition on commerce.
governorate—an Iraqi government administrative province.

Raising livestock was the way that most Kurds historically made their living. Even today, many Kurds in rural areas care for herds of sheep or goats.

Mining is a major industry in mineral-rich Kurdistan. Within the Zagros and Taurus ranges lie significant deposits of copper, chromium, iron ore, and coal. Quarries provide construction materials such as granite, limestone, marble, and travertine, as well as raw materials for cement factories.

But more important than mining is petroleum refinement. Rich oil reserves can be found throughout the Kurdish region—around the cities of Rumayla in Syria, Batman and Silvan in Turkey, and Kirkuk and Khaniqin in Iraq. As oil reserves in these regions have been developed, many Kurds have left their rural villages to work as unskilled laborers in the petroleum refineries.

POVERTY AND PROGRESS

In theory, Kurdistan's many natural resources—fertile soil, abundant water, and rich mineral reserves—should provide its people with a healthy economy. However, for most of the Kurds' history, other powers have exploited the region's most lucrative resources. As a result, the majority of Kurds in Turkey, Syria, and Iran live in poverty. In most villages, one or two wealthy families own most of the land that is good for farming or for pasturing livestock. The rest of the villagers own either plots just large enough for subsistence farming or no land at all. Landless townspeople usually work as unskilled laborers or as herders for wealthy landowners.

Some Kurdish political groups blame the poverty of the Kurds on the governments of Turkey, Syria, and Iran, claiming they have deliberately chosen not to invest in regions with large Kurdish populations. In all three nations, the public services, infrastructure, education, and health care in Kurdish areas are drastically underdeveloped, especially when compared to areas with predominantly Arab and Turkish populations.

In Turkey, the Kurds' economic situation is also blamed on the years of warfare between the government and the PKK, which has devastated the agricultural economy of the southeastern region. The hundreds of thousands of Kurds displaced by warfare from their villages in Turkey received no foreign aid or government financial assistance. Because of the high poverty rate and massive unemployment in rural areas, many Kurds have moved to cities in search of work.

In Iraq, however, the Kurdish people have fared better than their neighbors. The creation of the no-fly zone over northern Iraq in 1991 promised security and stability, although Iraqi Kurds did not experience economic progress until the late 1990s. Earlier in the decade, they had suffered financial hardships because of the international trade **embargo** imposed on Iraq after the first Persian Gulf War. These economic sanctions were established to punish Iraq for refusing to comply with postwar agreements, which included the disarmament of its weapons program. The economy of Iraqi Kurdistan also struggled because of ongoing warfare between the two major Kurdish factions. Economic growth became attainable only after the KDP and PUK made peace in 1998.

Iraqi Kurdistan also benefited greatly from the United Nations (U.N.) oil-for-food program, instituted in December 1996. The program allowed the Iraqi government in Baghdad to export a limited amount of oil, but the money from oil sales could be used only for the purchase of humanitarian supplies such as food, medicine, and other nonmilitary goods. A portion of the revenue from Iraq's oil sales—13 percent—was allocated specifically for the Kurdish northern region. The Kurds desperately needed the money to rebuild the thousands of villages destroyed by the Baathist government. The stream of Kurdish refugees returning home from Iran to the protection of the no-fly zone also needed housing and food.

U.N. administrators used oil-for-food money to build roads and bridges, houses, schools, health clinics, water and sewerage systems, irrigation networks, and electricity and running water projects in the region. Money from the program and assistance from other small nongovernmental relief organizations (NGOs) also provided medical care such as vaccinations and the distribution of medical supplies to hospitals and clinics. Oil-for-food revenue helped with the massive job of clearing an estimated 12 to 15 million land mines from fields in Iraqi Kurdistan. To ensure that no one went hungry, the U.N. also established a policy that every inhabitant of the north, regardless of income, received a monthly food basket.

Despite the embargo, some diesel fuel and crude oil were illegally smuggled out of Iraq by caravans of trucks traveling through northern Iraq to Turkey. The Kurdistan Democratic Party imposed "tariffs" on oil smugglers at border crossings, and used the revenue to administer the region. Money went for the construction of schools, roads, and hospitals within Kurdistan, and paid the salaries of its militia, local police forces, and teachers.

In addition to the steady revenue from oil, Iraqi Kurdistan attracted private outside investment as well. The region saw a boom in construction projects such as shopping malls, hotel complexes, and an international airport. By 2002 northern Iraq could boast of bustling cities featuring Internet cafes and shopping bazaars that

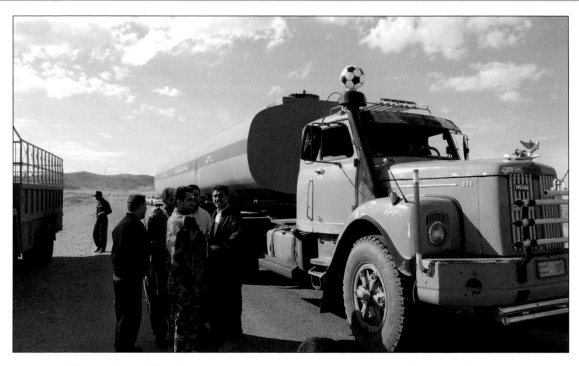

Officials of Iraqi Kurdistan stop a truck to search for contraband at a checkpoint near Chamchamal, northern Iraq. Revenue collected from truckers illegally smuggling Iraqi oil to Turkey was used to help finance the government of Iraqi Kurdistan.

sold CDs, computers, and cell phones as well as carpets, fruits, and vegetables. According to the Ministry of Reconstruction and Development, between 1992 and 2002 more than half of the 4,000 villages destroyed under Iraq's Baath regime had been rebuilt.

After the 2003 Persian Gulf War, the oil embargo against Iraq was lifted and the oil-for-food program was discontinued, although the Kurds were given former U.N. property such as cars, computers, and power plants as compensation for the program's termination. Around the same time the U.S. Coalition Authority banned oil smuggling and toll and tariff collections at the borders, which had accounted for most of the regional government's revenue. To replace this income, the Kurdistan Regional Government received funding from the U.S.-backed government—enough money to allow the Kurdish government to quadruple the salaries of its employees and militia. Today, Kurdistan is one of Iraq's more prosperous regions. However, disputes over oil revenue have caused economic, and political, deadlock. Under the constitution, the central government pays the KRG 17% of the nation's oil income, but the payments have frequently been delayed and reduced. These payments constitute the majority of the KRG's budget and it has been unable to pay government workers for extended periods. This situation, combined with the violence and uncertainty of the ISIL invasion, have led to a large budget deficit for the KRG.

KURDISH POLITICS IN TURKEY

The violent methods of the Kurdistan Workers Party (PKK), which sought an independent Kurdish state, did not appeal to many Kurds living in Turkey. An outlawed organization, the PKK financed its operations by illegal activities such as the smuggling of drugs and humans. Most Kurds in Turkey preferred to work within the nation's political system to gain recognition of their civil rights. But such efforts were often difficult. Turkish authorities jailed many Kurdish teachers and politicians for advocating for the right to speak and teach in their native tongue.

During the 1990s four pro-Kurdish political parties, all calling for laws that guaranteed equal rights for Kurds, were banned in succession. In 1991, several Kurdish deputies (officials elected to Turkey's National Assembly) formed the People's Labor Party (Halkin Emek Partisi, or HEP); within two years, Turkey's Constitutional Court had declared the fledgling party illegal. The deputies then formed a new political party with similar goals, called the Democracy Party (Demokrasi Partisi, or DEP). By 1994, DEP was banned, and several of its supporters jailed. Next came the People's Democratic Party (Halkin Demokrasi Partisi, or HADEP), which, after it was banned in 1999, changed its name to the

Democratic People's Party, or DEHAP.

In 2005, DEHAP leaders announced that the party was merging with another Kurdish group to form the new Democratic Society Party (Demokratik Toplum Partisi, or DTP). The DTP also faced accusations of collaborating with the PKK and was banned in 2009. Today, the pro-Kurdish party is called the People's Democracy Party.

Over the years a number of Kurds have been leaders in the Turkish government, holding high positions as foreign ministers or even prime ministers. However, those who scaled the ranks in Turkish government and society often did so because they deliberately did not identify themselves as Kurds. In fact, many Kurds, especially those who live in the western cities or who have married Turks, do not consider ethnic identity in politics and do not vote exclusively for the Kurdish party.

The PKK officially ended its ceasefire in 2003, returning to a campaign of frequent attacks. Typically, police officers are targeted, but civilians and tourists have also been killed. Turkish forces attacked suspected PKK bases in Iraqi Kurdistan in 2007, 2008, and 2012. In 2014, PKK fighters fired at a Turkish outpost in Hakkari from across the Iraq border and the Turkish military retaliated.

KURDISH POLITICS IN IRAQ

Iraq's autonomous Kurdish region consists of the three northern **governorates** (provinces) of Iraq: Erbil, Dahuk, and as-Sulaymaniyah. In May 1992, the Kurds living there elected a joint 105-member representative regional assembly, a parliament that met in the city of Erbil. This assembly consisted of 50 members from each of the two major parties (the KDP and PUK), and in an effort to establish equal rights for minorities (including the Turkmen, Assyrians, Chaldeans, and Arabs), the assembly also included five representatives from minority parties.

The new government announced the creation of a Kurdish administration, the Kurdish Regional Government (KRG), that ultimately had two administrations, two prime ministers, and two militias. The KDP government, headed by Massoud Barzani and based in the city of Erbil, controlled the rural northwestern regions, while the PUK government, led by Jalal Talabani, administered the more urban southeastern lands from its base in as-Sulaymaniyah.

The most widely used version of the Kurdish flag consists of a yellow sun placed between bands of red, white, and green. The golden sun disk, an ancient Kurdish symbol, emblazons the center. From the time of the Ottoman Empire, Kurdish groups have raised this flag in defiance against oppressive rule.

Although friction between the two major parties resulted in civil war from 1994 to 1998, by 2002 Iraqi Kurdistan had made great gains and could boast of many features similar to that of an independent nation: it had three universities, more than 50 newspapers and magazines, two satellite television stations and numerous radio stations, and a Kurdish school curriculum, not to mention its own Kurdish army and flag. Because the region was still part of Iraq, its government used Iraqi passports (that the KRG government processed) and currency (Iraqi dinars that the KRG had printed in Switzerland).

In June 2003, after the second Gulf War was declared over, the two separate KDP and PUK governments agreed to create a unified Kurdish government. The KDP prime minister, Nechirvan Barzani, Massoud's nephew, became the KRG prime minister. Both Massoud

Barzani and Talabani, along with three other Kurds, were appointed to the 25-member Iraqi Governing Council set up by the U.S.-run Coalition Provisional Authority. The coalition government also included five ministries run by Kurds, including water and foreign affairs.

Although other Iraqi militias were banned after the end to hostilities was declared, the KDP and PUK were allowed to keep their *peshmerga* armies, intelligence forces, and prisons. (Kurdish militiamen now wear the Iraqi army uniform, but many feature a Kurdish flag patch on the shoulder.) However, the separate Kurdish currency was abolished as of January 2004, having been replaced by the new Iraqi dinar in October 2003.

In March 2004, the Iraqi Governing Council officially approved the interim Iraqi constitution. The preliminary constitution established the Presidency Council, consisting of a president and two deputy presidents. To attain equal representation, these three positions had to be filled by one Shiite Arab, one Sunni Arab, and one Sunni Kurd. In turn, the Presidency Council would appoint a prime minister, members of a council of ministers, and a nine-member federal Supreme Court for Iraq.

The interim constitution allowed minority groups such as Kurds and Sunni Arabs to veto the permanent constitution. In other words, they have the right to object to any law—a provision that was opposed by the majority Shiite leaders. The document also affirmed that the Iraqi Kurds would keep their regional government, elected assembly, and police. Kurdish was also listed as an official language of Iraq.

In June 2004, a new interim government replaced the Iraqi Governing Council. The high-ranking positions of vice president and deputy national security prime minister went to Kurdish leaders. The new cabinet elected Jalal Talabani president in April 2005. Two months later, Massoud Barzani became president of the new

KRG. Barzani was reelected in 2009, and in 2013 the Kurdish Parliament extended his term to 2015.The National Assembly drafted a permanent constitution in 2005, confirming Kurdish semi-autonomy in Dahuk, Erbil, and as-Sulaymaniyah. The constitution was ratified in a national referendum in October of that year, supported by most Kurdish voters.

In May 2006, the KRG formally introduced its cabinet, which divided power between the KDP and PUK. In the 2013 parliamentary elections, the KDP won the most votes at 38 percent. The PUK is waning in popularity and received only 18 percent. Gorran, an offshoot of the PUK, gained power with 24 percent of the vote. Today, the Kurdish parliament has 111 elected members, 30 percent of which are women. Minorities, such as Turkomen, Assyrians, and Armenians also hold some seats in parliament.

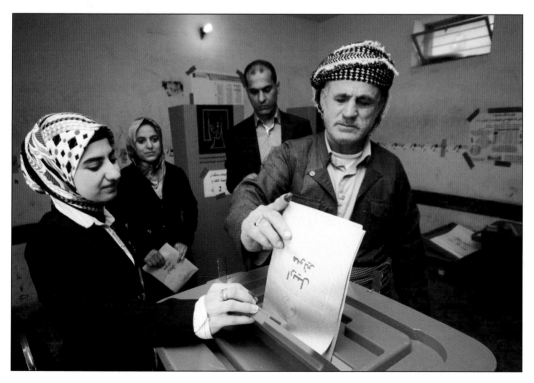

A Kurdish man votes in the Iraqi general election in 2014. Residents of Kurdistan also vote for their regional leaders.

Nechirvan Barzani was elected prime minister of Iraqi Kurdistan in 2012. He is a nephew of the regional president, Massoud Barzani.

KURDISH POLITICS IN IRAN AND SYRIA

Iran is an Islamic republic with a Shiite majority. Among the armed political groups opposing the government is the Democratic Party of Iranian Kurdistan (KDPI), a nationalist movement that has been pushed into northern Iraq. This is territory controlled by Iraq's PUK, which has received support in the past from the Iranian government. Although both the PUK and KDPI are Kurdish groups, the PUK has remained separate from the KDPI and has even attempted to prevent it from using Iraq as a base to launch attacks on Iran.

In general, Iranian Kurds can participate in politics; some have even become members of parliament. However, before the spring 2004 elections the Iranian government disqualified candidates who were pushing for reforms, and many of them were Kurds. Some analysts believe this crackdown occurred because of government concerns over the large public celebrations in Iran that accompanied the March 2004 approval of Iraq's interim constitution, a document that essentially granted autonomy to Iraqi Kurds. The

Iranian government continues to limit Kurdish freedoms and has jailed, tortured, and executed Kurdish activists.

Although Kurds in Syria cannot legally form political parties, some operate within the one-party system of the National Progressive Front (NPF). Some Kurds have attained membership in parliament, but have limited powers. The Kurdish Leadership Console in Western Kurdistan (KLC) is a group that represents major Kurdish groups and tribal leaders working to achieve cultural and political rights for Syrian Kurds.

RELIGION

Most Kurds (about 75 to 85 percent) are Sunni Muslims, which is also the majority faith in Turkey. As many as 15 percent of Kurds belong to the Shia sect of Islam, the predominant faith in Iraq and Iran. Most Shiite Kurds live in Iran, where they make up about one-fourth of the Iranian Kurdish population.

The Islamic faith dictates much of the way of life for its followers by establishing a specific code of behavior, ethics, and habits. Among the practices of the devout Muslim is praying five times a day while facing Mecca, the birthplace of the religion's founder, the prophet Muhammad.

A majority of Kurds also participate in one of many mystical Islamic sects called Sufi orders, or *tariqa*. Major Sufi orders include the Bektashi in northwest Kurdistan, Naqshbandi in western and northern Kurdistan, Kadiri in eastern and central Kurdistan, and Nurbakhshi in southern Kurdistan. The holy men of different *tariqa* orders are called *sheikhs* (also spelled *shaykhs*). Sufi practices involve many non-Islamic rites and rituals,

 Did You Know?

A small number of Kurds who follow the Jewish faith once lived in southern regions of Kurdistan; they migrated to Israel during the 1950s.

A Kurdish man prays on the roof of the historic temple of Yezidis in the village of Lalesh, Iraq. There are about 300,000 Yezidis worldwide, most of whom are Kurds who live in northern Iraq, Iran, Turkey, Syria, the former Soviet Union, and western Europe (particularly Germany).

such as meditation, trances, ecstatic utterances, and self-mutilation (such as piercing the skin with daggers or skewers). Such mystical practices are performed to attain communion with God, but they often offend strictly orthodox Muslims.

A minority of Kurds are neither Sunni nor Shia Muslims. A few follow the Christian faith. The rest belong to one of three religions referred to as the Cult of Angels because their followers believe in the existence of seven divine angels as well as one God. Two Cult of Angels religions draw upon the principles of the Shia Islam: the Alevis (4 million Kurds), who live mostly in eastern Turkey, and the Ahl-e Haqq (about 1 million Kurds), who reside mostly near the

Iran-Iraq border. Turks, Arabs, and other ethnic groups besides Kurds practice the Alevi Muslim and Ahl-e Haqq faiths.

The small faction of believers in Yezidism, the third faith in the Cult of Angels, is made up exclusively of Kurds. Yezidism has been referred to as the original Kurdish religion because of its ancient origins. The religion combines pre-Islamic beliefs adopted from Zoroastrianism (a Persian religion founded between 1000 and 700 BCE) as well as aspects of Christianity, Judaism, and Sufism. Yezidis pray three times a day, while facing the sun. Numbering about 300,000, they live mostly in northern Iraq.

Text-Dependent Questions

1. What are the two main cash crops of Kurdistan?
2. Name three factors that lead to poverty in Kurdistan.
3. How does the 2005 Iraqi constitution affect Iraqi Kurds?

Research Project

Use a library or the Internet to research the oil deposits of Kurdistan. Learn where oil reserves are located, what income they bring to the country they are located in, and how they have played a role in the Kurdish independence movement.

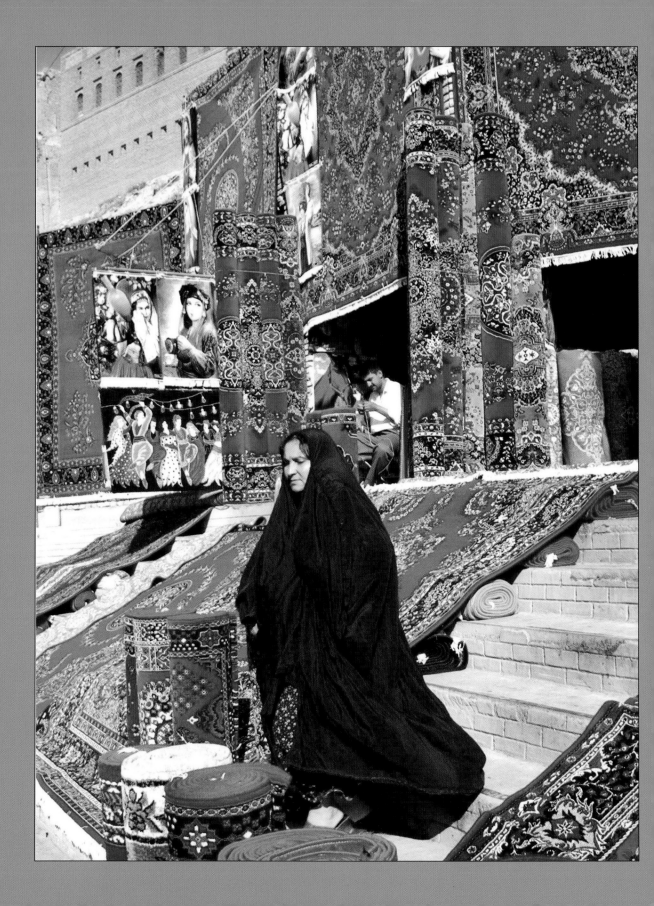

\A Kurdish woman, wearing a traditional garment called an *abaya*, walks down the steps of a carpet shop in Erbil, Iraq. The Kurds have a reputation for weaving intricate patterns into richly colored rugs called *kilims*.

The People

Since the 1960s the numbers of Kurds in the Middle East have been steadily growing, and today they represent about 15 percent of the region's population. However, because the nations in which Kurds live often do not identify them as a separate ethnic group in census surveys, reliable statistical information is hard to come by.

THE TRIBAL IDENTITY

Before the 1980s, Kurdish society was mainly rural and people lived in small villages scattered over the mountainsides. However, groups of villages remained connected with one other because their inhabitants belonged to the same tribe and followed the same leader. Tribes are groups of several families whose many members share a common ancestor and ownership of lands. Kurdish tribes established claim to certain lands, or the rights to use pasturelands owned by other tribes.

Did You Know?

The Kurds of Iran speak three major Kurdish dialects—Kermanji in Western Azerbaijan, Sorani in Kurdistan, and Gourani in Bakhtaran (spoken by the Hawraman tribe).

Ultimate control of territory traditionally lay with the tribal leader to whom Kurds gave absolute loyalty. In the past, this tribal chief, or *agha*, had absolute power, although today he serves mostly as a representative and advisor for his people. The tribal leader settles disputes, allocates land and water use, and maintains order over the villages within his jurisdiction, often with the aid of a council. Villages pay taxes to the *agha* in the form of cash or produce. Kurdish lands also may be controlled by religious leaders, or *sheikhs*, who serve the role of tribal chiefs. Individual villages are led by the *mukhtar*, or village chief.

Some Kurdish tribes are actually coalitions—groups of people of different ancestry who have banded together to form an entire tribe. Loyalty to the tribe and its chief is of utmost important to traditional, rural Kurds, although groups may change their allegiances. In many cases, tribes form their own regional political groups. Although the *agha* is not as powerful as he was in the past, many Kurds prefer to give him their trust and obedience rather than deal with state authorities.

Tribal identity is not as important to Kurds living in villages and cities, particularly those who have assimilated into non-Kurdish cities such as Istanbul and Tehran. However, many rural Kurds

Word to Understand in This Chapter

Ramadan—the ninth month of the Islamic calendar.
vernal equinox—the time during spring, around March 20 or 21, when the day and night are equal length.

Quick Facts: The Kurdish People

Total Population: 25 to 30 million.*
   Turkey: 14.7 million (18 percent of the population).
   Iraq: 4.9–6.5 million (15–20 percent).
   Iran: 8.8 million (10 percent).
   Syria: less than 1.7 million (under 10 percent).
Religion: Sunni Muslim, 75–85 percent; Shia Muslim, 15 percent; other faiths include Yezidism, Ahl-e Haqq, Alevi, and Christianity.
Languages: Kurdish; major dialects are Kermanji, Sorani, Gourani, and Zaza.

*These figures are estimates. Exact population figures are unavailable because the Turkish, Iraqi, Iranian, and Syrian governments have not conducted a reliable census of the Kurdish people living in their respective countries.
Source: Adapted from CIA World Factbook, 2015.

consider loyalty to their particular tribe and tribal leader of the highest importance.

LANGUAGE AND LITERATURE

The Kurdish language differs markedly from Turkish and Arabic. As an Indo-European language similar to Persian, it is closer to English, French, and German. Kurdish exists in many different dialects. Most Kurds speak one of two major dialects: Kermanji (also called Northern Kurdish or Kurmanci) and Sorani (Southern Kurdish). Kermanji is spoken by Kurds living in Turkey, in far northern Iraq (north of the Greater Zab River), and in parts of northern Iran, Syria, Armenia, and Georgia. Sorani is spoken by Iraqi Kurds living south of the Greater Zab and in much of Iran.

Other dialects include Zaza, spoken by Kurds living in northeastern Turkey and parts of northern Iran; and Gourani, spoken in parts of southern Iran. Speakers of northern and southern Kermanji can usually understand one another, but some Kurdish dialects differ so much their speakers cannot effectively communicate. More educated Kurds are usually bilingual, and in addition to

Kurdish speak Turkish in Turkey, Farsi in Iran, or Arabic in Iraq or Syria.

Both Zaza and Gourani are spoken dialects only, while the Kermanji and Sorani dialects are written as well as spoken. The alphabet used to write in Kurdish differs by country: in Turkey, the Latin alphabet is used; in the former Soviet Union, it is the Cyrillic alphabet; and in Iraq and Syria, Kurdish writings are in a modified form of Arabic. Thus, Kermanji is usually written in Latin script, while Sorani is written in modified Arabic script.

The first written history of the Kurdish people, called *Sharafnama*, was penned by Prince Sharaf al-Din Bitlisi in 1597. The book, whose title means "book of princes," describes the histories of the various Kurdish tribes. The author, born in a ruling family in northern Kurdistan, detailed many aspects of the Kurdish culture as well as the impact that different empires had on the people.

Kurdish children attend the public school in Mus, Turkey. Although some Kurdish families have sought to receive an education in their native language, the government does not permit public school instruction to be conducted in a language other than Turkish.

Kurdish literature largely consists of epic poems and tales of folklore, and many of them deal with heroism, romance, and the love of country. The poet Ahmad Khani (1651–1707) is said to have inspired Kurdish nationalism in 1695 with his epic *Mem o Zin*. This 17th-century poem tells of the doomed love between two young people of different tribes: a boy named Mem and girl named Zin who is already betrothed to another. Along with being a romantic tale, the poem celebrates Kurdish culture, discusses the Kurds' place among nations, and indicates a desire for self-governance that existed even then. The following excerpt from *Mem o Zin* reflects the poet's sentiment that Kurdish oppression will end:

> Look! Our misfortune has reached its zenith,
> Has it started to come down do you think?
> Or will it remain so,
> Until comes upon us the end of time?
> Is it possible, I wonder, that for us too,
> A star will emerge out of the firmament?
> Let luck be on our side for once.

Kurdish-language publications were prohibited by the Ottoman empire. To circumvent this ban, the first Kurdish-language newspaper was published outside Kurdistan—in Cairo, Egypt, in 1898. Because Syria and Turkey, where the Kermanji dialect is spoken, outlawed Kurdish-language publications for so many years, much modern Kurdish literature has been written in Sorani. In fact, during the 20th century more than 80 percent of all Kurdish books published were written in Sorani.

EDUCATION

Kurds living in Iraq have had the best opportunities to learn the Kurdish language in government-run schools, but only since the establishment of self-government in 1992. Early in Saddam Hussein's rule, the Iraqi government made some concessions to

Kurdish demands and permitted the founding of the School for Kurdish Studies at Baghdad University and the establishment of a Kurdish branch at the University of Sulaymaniyah. However, children in the government-run schools were educated only in Arabic.

After 1992, when an autonomous regional government assumed control over Iraqi Kurdistan, children under 10 were no longer taught in Arabic, but in Kurdish instead. Although some Kurds point with pride to this achievement, others remain concerned that this younger Kurdish-educated generation may have problems in the future because they will be unfamiliar with the Arabic that their neighbors speak.

Turkey has allowed Kurdish-language schools since 2003, but the legislation applies only to private schools. The language is not taught in the government-supported public schools. Today, only a small number of Kurds in Turkey can read and write in Kurdish because the language was outlawed for so long.

Some private schools and universities in Iran offer courses on the Kurdish culture and language; however, the language is not taught in the schools. Syria does not allow Kurdish to be spoken in any public gatherings, including schools.

MARRIAGE AND FAMILY LIFE

In strictly traditional Kurdish households, it is understood that Kurds must marry Kurds, and it is not unusual for extended family members such as cousins to wed. As is common in other parts of the Middle East, parents usually arrange marriages. In some cases, men who have gone abroad for study or work will come back home when it is time to marry and select from the prospects chosen by their mothers.

For traditional Kurds, arranged marriages involve an elaborate negotiation process. After the woman agrees to marry the man, his family makes a formal request. Then both families discuss the con-

Members of a Kurdish family celebrate a wedding.

ditions and bride-price, which is paid by the groom's family as gold, money, or property. In Kurdish society, gold and silver jewelry is a sign of wealth. The groom's family hosts the wedding, which can last two or three days and include hundreds of guests.

In accordance with Islamic law, men are expected to marry, and husbands may have more than one wife, particularly if the first marriage has not produced a son. In the past, large families with more than 10 children were typical in many Kurdish homes, and their extended families often numbered in the hundreds. Today, the typical family has three or four children.

In the strictly orthodox, or traditional, Muslim world, men and women must adhere to strict Islamic laws governing behavior and dress. For example, one of the tenets of Islam is showing proper hospitality. Visitors in a Kurdish household are warmly greeted with handshakes and offered candy, tea, and fruit. Kurds indicate their willingness to help someone by placing the hands over the

Did You Know?

For centuries, Kurds traditionally did not have last names, or surnames. They adopted last names only during the 20th century, when forced to do so by the governments of the nations in which they lived. Many Kurds followed the Arab tradition of taking their father's name as the middle name and the name of their tribe or region as the last name. Others took a grandfather's or great-grandfather's first name as their new surname.

eyes, and saying the common Kurdish expression *Ser chaow*, which literally means "on my eyes." This gesture and phrase simply mean "at your service."

Kurds tend to be more moderate than orthodox Muslims in their interpretations of Islamic law regarding acceptable behavior and dress for women. Kurdish women usually do not cover their faces or wear the *abaya* (or *chador*)—a long, black garment that orthodox Muslim women wear to completely cover the body. In most parts of Kurdistan, women can work outside the home: rural Kurdish women work in the fields, while many urban dwellers attend classes at schools and universities or work in businesses.

However, in more conservative parts of Iraqi Kurdistan, women are largely relegated to maintaining responsibility for the home. Most do not go out after 5 PM unless accompanied by their families; in Iraq's conservative cities women often do not go out by themselves at all. In rural parts of Kurdistan most women do not drive, travel by themselves, or spend the night away from home unless they are with male relatives. One's behavior reflects on the family, so most women feel bound to follow the dictates of the Kurdish society in which they live.

TRADITIONAL DRESS AND CUSTOMS

Traditional Kurdish clothes are colorful, sparkling with sequins and glittering gold and silver threads woven into bright fabrics. Patterns and colors vary according to the region and usually identify the wearer's tribe or political party. For example, the color of Iraq's PUK political party is yellow, while green identifies members of the KDP. Men of the Barzan region commonly sport turbans of red and white.

Kurdish men wear baggy trousers with a shirt and a short jacket, or *shalwar*. Together the trousers and jacket are called *shal u shapik*. An elaborately woven cummerbund (waistband) or decorative sash adorns the waist, and a skullcap and square of fabric tightly tied as a turban covers the head. The military-style *shal u shapik* is also known as *khak*.

The traditional dress for women also consists of loose trousers, but these are covered by a long, loose-fitting dress or caftan. To keep themselves warm, Kurdish women may wear several layers of dresses. A short vest often completes the outfit. Women also cover their head with a headscarf called a *sarbend*. In Turkey the women's headscarves are often edged with lace.

Kurdish everyday dress differs from one region to the next. Women in urban areas of Iran typically wear the *abaya* or *chador* on the city streets because it is required by the Islamic government. In Iraq, more traditional Kurdish women also wear the abaya, although the garment is seldom seen in Turkey. More conservative Kurdish women in Iran and Iraq cover their faces with a garment called a *kheli* whenever they are in public. At home many Kurdish women wear whatever they wish.

Some Kurds today follow Western fashion, and their clothing can range from knee- or calf-length skirts and blouses for women or a three-piece suit for men to T-shirts and jeans for

 Did You Know?

It was not until September 2003 that the Turkish law forbidding Kurds from giving their children Kurdish names was lifted. However, parents still cannot use any names that contain the letters q, x, and w, which are found in the Kurdish alphabet but not in the Turkish alphabet.

A group of Kurdish girls wear brightly colored traditional garments while walking to a picnic in the countryside of northern Iraq.

both. Many young people wear the traditional dress only for special occasions, while it is everyday attire for older generations. In Iran many Kurdish men typically wear Western clothes in public, but feel more comfortable in baggy Kurdish trousers at home.

A traditional piece of Kurdish jewelry is the *parang*. This style of jewelry, no longer in fashion, consists of many gold and silver coins on a chain that is worn around the neck or waist or along the brim of a hat or turban.

Music

The poetry of the Kurds often appears in their songs, and there are songs for every occasion. Some are featured only at special occasions, such as wedding or holiday celebrations. Others have religious ties; for example, some *gouranis* are sung in villages and cities during the Islamic month of **Ramadan** to herald the coming of dawn (when Muslims can have food before they begin their fast for the day). A funeral procession might be accompanied by the singing of *chemari gouranis*, sad songs that usually lament the loss of a young person.

Music is not just for special occasions, it is a part of everyday life. There are Kurdish lullabies, children's songs, and work songs. For instance, rural women working in the fields may sing traditional songs as they go about their chores of milking the cows or carrying water from the springs. Although the broadcast of Kurdish songs on television or the radio was banned for many years in Iraq, Iran, and Turkey, the music lived on, eventually making its way to Kurdistan via satellite television networks.

Singing is often accompanied by stringed instruments such as lutes (regional variations of the instrument include the *saz, tambur,* and *oud*); percussion instruments (*dehol,* a large cylindrical drum); and wind instruments such as oboes (*zurna, nerme ney, balaban*) and flutes (*shimshal* or *dudik*).

Playing instruments, singing songs, and line dancing enliven picnics, which are a common tradition in Kurdistan. Such events include setting up tents, building bonfires for barbecues, and sharing in the company of friends and family members while enjoying good food and drink.

CUISINE

The Kurdish diet consists mostly of vegetables and grains, although the Kurds eat lamb, mutton, and chicken as well as some beef. They prefer meat that has been butchered according to Islamic law so that it is halal, or pure. Islamic dietary laws forbid the consumption of pork, although wild pigs and boars are common in Kurdistan.

Meats are usually cooked in dishes with rice or bulgur (a kind of wheat) and vegetables, or they are simmered in rich stews. Among popular Kurdish dishes are *biryani* rice, made with raisins, nuts, and chicken; *tershick*, wheat patties filled with vegetables and lamb; and *dughabba*, wheat patties stuffed with ground lamb and served in a mint-flavored goat's milk broth.

Meals commonly include vegetables such as eggplant, summer squash, cucumbers, and tomatoes that have been flavored with salt, pepper, cumin, garlic, and cooking oil. Pomegranate juice is also a common ingredient in many Kurdish dishes. Fruits such as apricots, watermelon, and fresh or dried grapes may be offered to visiting guests as a snack or part of a meal.

An essential part of a Kurdish breakfast is *nan tanik* (large doughy flat bread that has been baked on a circular iron mound

Members of an extended Kurdish family eat dinner together at a home in Qamishli, Syria.

heated by coals). It is usually served with local white cheese that is made from curdled milk and flavored with herbs. It may be eaten with plain yogurt, honey, and tea.

A typical Middle Eastern drink, called *du*, consists of yogurt and water. Kurds commonly drink *chai*, a strongly sugared tea usually served in small, tulip-shaped glasses. Most Iranian Kurds drink *chai* Persian-style: with a sugar cube held in the mouth.

KURDISH FESTIVALS

The biggest festival for the Kurds, no matter what nation they live in, is Newroz, which means "new dawn" in Kurdish. For the Kurds, the first day of spring is the first day of the year, so the holiday is also referred to as the Kurdish New Year. Newroz falls during the ***vernal equinox***—around March 20th or 21st. Some believe the holiday had its origins in the Zoroastrian faith, an ancient religion more than 2,700 years old.

For the Kurds, the story behind Newroz is one of victory over tyranny. According to one Kurdish legend, a tyrannical Persian king named Rustom ruled over the Kurds about 2,500 years ago. One day, a young Kurdish ironsmith called Kawa decided to end Rustom's rule. He told his fellow Kurds that he would light a fire on the highest mountain peak as a signal that it was time for them all to attack the palace. The plan worked. The Kurds stormed the king's fortress, allowing Kawa to kill the ruthless dictator. Other versions of the story explain that news of the king's overthrow was spread to the rest of Kurdistan by people lighting signal fires, sending the word from mountaintop to mountaintop.

Kurds today celebrate the tyrant's defeat by lighting small bonfires in the streets and hills and jumping over them. Some believe the ritual of jumping over the flames cleanses them of impurities. During Newroz, families gather for picnics or visit with family and friends, sometimes exchanging small gifts.

Waving a red, gold, and green rope (the colors of the Kurdish flag), a woman dances with her husband inside a circle, with friends and neighbors clapping, at the annual Newroz celebration near the city of Diyarbakir in southeastern Turkey. Newroz celebrates the first day of spring and the first day of the Kurdish new year.

Newroz is a national holiday for all citizens of Iran, but it is a major holiday to the Kurds, who see it as a celebration of their nationality and culture. In Iraq's Kurdistan Region Newroz is an official three-day holiday. In Turkey the holiday has often been banned because the bonfire celebrations have led to violence between government authorities and ethnic Kurds.

As Muslims, Kurds also observe the major Islamic holidays. One of the most important is the Feast of the Sacrifice, or Eid al-Adha (also called Eid al-Qurban). This day celebrates the story told in the Qur'an of the patriarch Abraham's willingness to sacrifice his son Ishmael to Allah. Because Abraham obeyed God, the boy was spared and a ram was sacrificed in his place. Kurds celebrate Eid al-Adha with a ritual slaughter of a sheep or goat. Over a four-day-long festival, family and community members gather and feast together, and donate a portion of the meal to the poor.

A second feast, Eid al-Fitr, celebrates the end of Ramadan, the ninth month of the Islamic lunar calendar. During the month of Ramadan, adult Muslims refrain from eating and drinking during daylight hours. By fasting, they practice self-control and work to become more spiritual in their faith. They also develop a better compassion for those who are poor and must fast because they have no food. At sundown, faithful Muslims break their fast. At the end of Ramadan, they hold the major feast of Eid-al-Fitr to mark the end of the period of self-sacrifice.

 ## Text-Dependent Questions

1. Describe the role of the Kurdish tribal leader in modern times.
2. Describe a traditional Kurdish picnic.
3. What does the holiday of Newroz celebrate?

 ## Research Project

Use the Internet or a library to learn about Kurdish women leaders. Create an oral presentation about historical and modern-day women leaders in politics, religion, and the military.

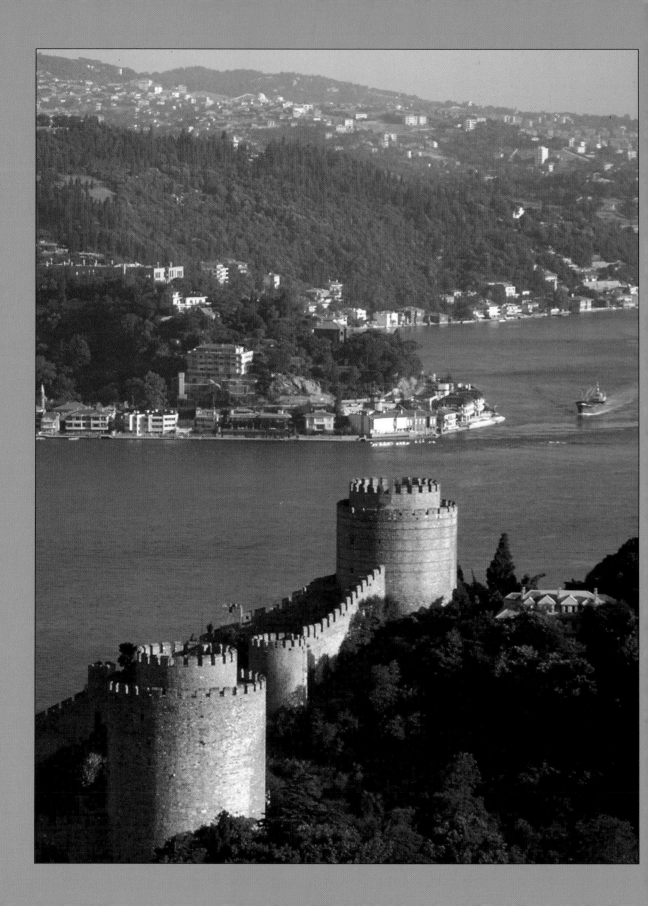

A view of Istanbul, the largest city in Turkey. More Kurds live in Istanbul than in any other city in the world.

Cities and Communities

Most Kurds today live in cities and villages instead of on farms. Forced evictions, warfare, and extreme poverty have pushed many rural Kurds to urban areas.

MAJOR KURDISH CITIES IN TURKEY

In Turkey, some Kurdish migrants moved to western cities with majority Turkish populations, such as Ankara and Istanbul. Others settled in large cities in southeastern Turkey, a region that has 10 Turkish provinces with majority Kurd populations. Many poor and homeless Kurds found shelter in shantytowns called *gecekondus* that sprang up on the edges of both Turkish and Kurdish cities.

The predominantly Turkish city of Istanbul has attracted Kurdish migrants for centuries. Approximately 3 million Kurds live in the city today, a much-larger Kurdish population than that of Diyarbakir, which is Turkey's largest city with majority Kurdish population.

Diyarbakir is the capital of the Turkish province bearing the same name. More than 1.5 million inhabitants live in this major urban center, the ninth largest in Turkey. Located in southeastern Turkey atop a plateau next to the Tigris River, the city was founded around 1500 BCE. It subsequently was ruled by Arabs, Seljuk Turks, and Persians before being conquered by the Ottoman Turks in 1515. During the 1990s and early 2000, more than 300,000 displaced Kurdish villagers fled to *gecekondus* that grew up around Diyarbakir, swelling its population to almost a million.

An ancient town, Diyarbakir contains many mosques and churches. The city features one of the oldest mosques in Turkey—the 11th century Ulu Mosque. Among the city's most striking landmarks are the black basalt ruins of fortress walls that encircle the town and date from the fourth century CE.

This Kurdish city is a trade center for agricultural crops such as grains, melons, and cotton, as well as for mineral products such as copper ore and petroleum—all of which are produced in the surrounding region. Major manufactures include flour, wine, textiles, and machinery. Diyarbakir also has an international airport and a major university.

Archeologists have found evidence that the city of Erzurum, located in eastern Turkey, existed during the fifth century CE. Then called Theodosiopolis, it served as an important Byzantine fortress. The city is celebrated by Turks as the site of the first national Turkish Congress, headed by Mustafa Kemal Atatürk in 1919.

 Words to Understand in This Chapter

caravan—a group of people traveling together, often carrying goods on a trade route.
gecekondus—shantytowns where the very poor live on the outskirts of Turkish cities.

Modern Erzurum claims a population of almost 400,000, which makes it the 21st-largest city in Turkey. Erzurum has a large Kurdish population. It serves as a major agricultural trade center for crops grown in the region, such as sugar beets, wheat, barley, and vegetables. Erzurum is also known for its metal and leather handicrafts, and is an important railroad center.

Located in eastern Turkey, Van sits along the edge of the country's largest lake, also called Van. The city dates to the 13th century BCE when it was founded as the capital of the kingdom of Urartu, or Ararat. During World War I, the town and surrounding region saw bitter fighting, as Turkish and Kurdish forces battled Armenians and Russians. Ultimately the original city of Van was destroyed by the Ottomans, after which it was captured by the Russians in 1915. Following the creation of the Turkish Republic in 1923, the government erected a new city of Van a few miles east of the original town.

Today Van, with a population over 387,000, is a predominantly Kurdish city that serves as a market center for local Kurdish farmers selling fruits and grains.

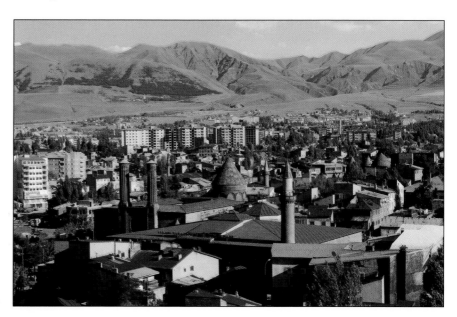

Erzurum, a city in eastern Turkey, was once an important stopping point on the trade routes that connected Asia and Europe. Today, it has a large Kurdish population.

MAJOR KURDISH CITIES IN IRAQ

The three largest cities within Iraqi Kurdistan have the same names as the governorates in which they are located: Erbil, as-Sulaymaniyah, and Dahuk. However, two other important cities of Iraq that the Kurds count as their own, but that also contain large numbers of other ethnic groups, are Mosul and Kirkuk.

Erbil (known as Hawler in Kurdish) is located in the southern part of the Kurdish autonomous region. It hosts a mostly Kurdish population of almost 1 million residents. The fourth-largest city in Iraq, Erbil is the country's second-largest predominantly Kurdish city.

One of the world's oldest continuously inhabited towns, Erbil was founded before 2300 BCE as the ancient Sumerian city of Urbilum. Later it served as an important trading center because of its strategic location along the **caravan** route between the cities of Baghdad and Mosul. Today, the city hosts the headquarters of the KDP and is the seat of the Kurdish parliament. It is also a major commercial and agricultural center.

During the 1990s, Erbil was devastated as the PUK and KDP fought for power in northern Iraq. Since 2000, the city has seen significant rebuilding as well as new construction. It now features a

The government of the Iraqi Kurdistan Region is located in Erbil.

Kurdish studies academy, the Iraq Institute of Democracy, Salahaddin University, and parks with amphitheaters for musical performances. The newly constructed Hawler International Airport opened in June 2003.

The sixth-largest city in Iraq and the nation's second-largest Kurdish city, Sulaymaniyah is home to more than 725,000 residents. It is a relatively young city, compared with many of its neighbors, having been founded around 1785 by the Baban princes (one of the most influential Kurdish dynasties), who made it the capital of their emirate. In 1919, Sheikh Mahmoud Barzinji led the first of many uprisings against the British here, and in 1923 declared it part of his newly formed kingdom of Kurdistan. British bombs forced him out of the city, but he continued to fight from the mountains until 1927.

Sulaymaniyah lies in northeastern Iraq, near the border with Iran. It has been under the jurisdiction of the PUK since 1991, and refugee camps on the city's outskirts have served as a safe haven for many displaced Kurds.

The first Kurdish press was established in as-Sulaymaniyah in 1920, and the city has since remained a center for Kurdish publishing. Today, with its numerous offices and hotels, as-Sulaymaniyah serves as an important trade and administrative center for the Kurdish autonomous region. The first Kurdish school of higher education, the University of Sulaymaniyah, was founded here in 1968.

The major urban center of Dahuk serves the provinces along the Turkish border. Traditionally under the jurisdiction of the KDP, Dahuk has a predominantly Kurdish population of approximately 200,000. In downtown Dahuk stands the Institute of Fine Arts and the University of Dahuk, both founded in 1992, after the area fell under the protection of the no-fly zone.

Located in the Ninawa governorate, Mosul has a population of approximately 1.5 million, making it the largest city of Iraqi Kurdistan and one of the largest cities in Iraq.

Because of its strategic location on the Tigris River, Mosul was an important commercial trade center of the region from the 8th to the 13th centuries. It was particularly known for its fine-quality cotton goods, called muslin, a fabric named for the city. Mosul was also renowned for its fine marble.

The discovery and subsequent development of oil reserves in the region surrounding Mosul have made the province immensely valuable. The region was occupied by the British following World War I, and soon afterward became part of the British mandate of Iraq. The Kurdish people continue to claim the land for their own, as does the Turkish Republic and the people in southern Iraq.

Mosul's population is mostly Arab, although the surrounding region is inhabited mainly by Kurds. The city lost much of its Kurdish population during the 1970s and 1980s through Saddam Hussein's Arabization program, when Kurds were forced from the region, although many later returned.

Mosul serves as an agricultural trade center for regional crops and livestock. It is also a manufacturing center for oil, cement, and textiles. Railroads link the city to major cities within Iraq, while roads connect the city with Turkey. Mosul is also home to Mosul University.

Mosul has been one of the least stable cities since the U.S. invasion in 2003. In June 2014 the Islamic State took over the city as it swept through northern Iraq. *Peshmerga* fighters have gained some ground against ISIL in the surrounding area, but as of May 2015 had not been able to retake the city, despite assistance from the United States that included airstrikes and military supplies.

Located about 90 miles (145 km) south of Mosul, Kirkuk lies within the at-Ta'mim governorate of Iraq. With a population of more than 975,000, Kirkuk is Iraq's fifth-largest city.

In 1934, development of Kirkuk's oil field began, and the city quickly became an important center of the petroleum industry. Two parallel oil pipelines, built in 1977 and 1987, carry oil from Kirkuk to the port city of Ceyhan, Turkey, on the Mediterranean Sea. The region in and around the city is Iraq's largest oil producer. Oil analysts estimate that Kirkuk has reserves of approximately 8.7 billion barrels, or as much as 40 percent of the oil reserves of Iraq. Besides serving as a major oil producer, Kirkuk is also a trade center for the region's agriculture, with major crops such as cereals, olives, fruits, and cotton. The city is also home to some textile manufacturing.

The Kurds consider Kirkuk their economic and cultural center, and those who propose an independent Kurdish state would like to see it as the capital. However, the city is located outside the Kurdish autonomous region, just to its south, and Arabs, Assyrian Christians, and Turkomen (an ethnic group related to the Turks) also claim the city as their own.

Much of Kirkuk's heavily Kurdish and Turkomen ethnic population changed during the 1970s and 1980s because of Saddam Hussein's Arabization programs. During the 2003 Persian Gulf War in Iraq, Kurdish forces captured the city. This power shift resulted in a mass migration of Arabs from Kirkuk, as well as a return of its Kurdish population. However, ethnic tensions, riots, and occasional violent attacks between Arabs, Turkomen, and Kurds continue to devastate the city. Following the 2003 Gulf War, Kurdish leaders continued to keep a strong presence in Kirkuk. In June 2003, the Shafaq cultural center, which celebrates the Kurdish language and culture, opened in the city.

After the Islamic State's capture of Mosul, ISIL attacked Kirkuk. The Iraqi army fell apart and fled, a repeat of the Mosul battle. However, this time the central government gave the *peshmerga* permission to engage and they quickly retook the city and saved Kirkuk from ISIL occupation.

MAJOR KURDISH CITIES IN IRAN AND SYRIA

Most Iranian Kurds live in the western part of the country, in the midst of the Zagros mountain range that runs parallel to the borders of Turkey and Iraq. The three mostly Kurdish areas are found in parts of the province of West Azerbaijan, the province of Kordestan (Kurdistan), and all of the province of Bakhtaran (formerly known as Kermanshah).

During the 1970s, many rural Iranian Kurds migrated from their villages to traditionally Kurdish cities such as Bakhtaran, Sanandaj, and Mahabad. Other Kurds settled in Iran's large non-Kurdish cities, such as Tabriz and Tehran. As a result, about two-thirds of Iranian Kurds now live in large towns and cities.

The ninth-largest city in Iran, with a population of over 800,000, Bakhtaran is the capital of the province of the same name, which is the southernmost province in Iran. As an ancient city, it was named Kermanshah and was founded in the fourth century CE by the Sassanids. The Arabs captured the city in the seventh century, as did the Ottoman Turks during World War I. The name was changed from Kermanshah to Bakhtaran in 1979, at the time of the Islamic Revolution.

Bakhtaran is an important commercial center for agricultural products, such as grain, rice, vegetables, fruits, and oilseed, all of which come from the fertile lands of the surrounding region. The city is also an important manufacturing center, producing textiles and carpets; refined sugar and other processed foods; and refined petroleum.

Unofficially referred to as "Iran's Kurdish capital," Sanandaj officially serves as the capital of the Kordestan province, in western Iran. Formerly known as Sinneh, Sanandaj is located in western Iran, close to the border with Iraq, and boasts a mostly Kurdish, Sorani-speaking population of over 370,000. The city is Iran's 22nd largest.

During the 19th century Sanandaj was the center for the production of Senneh *kilims*, finely woven carpets with bold bright designs crafted by Kurdish weavers. During the 1979 revolution, the city was also the scene of many battles between Kurdish rebels and the Islamic Revolution Guard. Sanandaj continues to be a site of Kurdish unrest.

Besides its famous *kilims*, Sanandaj and the surrounding region is also known for fine handicrafts such as woodwork, metalwork, and needlework. The city serves as a trade center for agricultural produce and features light industries such as textile manufacturing (carpets), tanning of hides and skins, rice milling, and sugar refining.

Located in West Azerbaijan, the historically Kurdish city of Mahabad served as the capital of the short-lived Kurdish nation of the same name, which was established in 1946. Almost 150,000 Iranians call Mahabad their home.

A large number of Kurds live on the outskirts of the Syrian capital, Damascus, in a section known as Hayy al Akrad (Quarter of the Kurds). Other groups live in the northeastern and northwestern parts of al-Jazirah and in the foothills of Kurd Dagh. Qamishli, located in the al-Jazira region, is home to a mixture of ethnic groups, including Kurds, Arabs, Turks, and Assyrians.

Text-Dependent Questions

1. Which Turkish city has the largest population of Kurds?
2. What city is in Iraq's largest oil-producing region?
3. What city is called Iran's unofficial Kurdish capital?

Research Project

Use the Internet or a library to learn about the history of Erbil, Iraq. Create a timeline of major events that includes ancient history, changes in ruling powers, and events as part of Iraq and Iraqi Kurdistan.

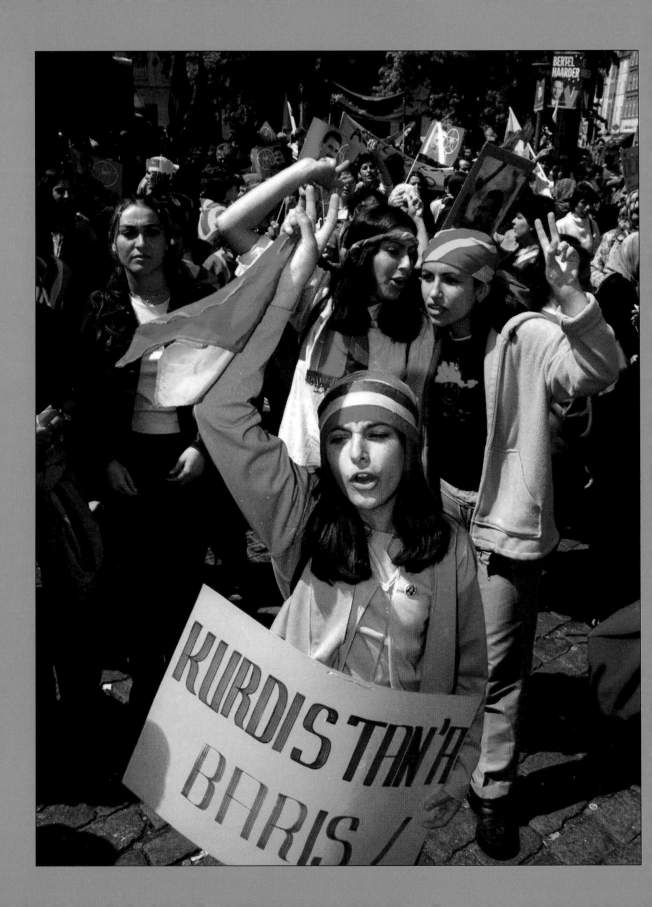

Kurdish demonstrators protest during a rally in Copenhagen, Denmark. The persecution that Kurds have endured in their traditional Middle Eastern homeland has forced many Kurds to immigrate to Europe, the United States, and other countries.

Foreign Relations

O ver the past century Kurds have appealed to foreign nations for help in obtaining civil rights in Turkey, Iraq, Iran, and Syria. Too often, Kurds say, their requests have fallen on deaf ears. Many Kurdish people believe that history has shown an old Kurdish proverb to be true: "The Kurds have no friends but the mountains."

KURDS AROUND THE WORLD

Exposure to Western ideas through the Internet and television has motivated many Kurds, especially young people, to search for a new life outside Kurdistan. Others have tired of living in areas where they cannot find jobs or where friends and family are jailed or killed for trying to speak in their native tongue. Subsequently, there has been a vast Kurdish *diaspora*, or scattering of people who have settled in regions far from their homeland. Approximately 1.5 million Kurds live in Europe, with the majority (about 1 million) settled in Germany. Another 9,000 ethnic Kurds live in Canada and anywhere between 25,000 and 55,000 live in the United States. Although many Kurds have left the physical region of Kurdistan, they say the nation still lives in their hearts.

Some Kurds have left the region illegally, by working with human smuggling organizations that charge as much as $7,000 to **smuggle** immigrants into Europe. These arrangements involve setting up airline flights and helping with forged documents. Less expensive methods of leaving the country illegally are much more dangerous, and would-be immigrants often find themselves packed into the suffocating holds of trucks or boats with no food and little air. Those who risk leaving the country by crossing over the mountains during winter months face possible death from the harsh journey's freezing temperatures.

TURKISH KURDS AND THE EUROPEAN UNION

The one and a half million Kurds living in European countries have been vocal in their criticisms of Turkey for its oppression of the nation's Kurds. And Europeans have exerted pressure on Turkey to make reforms since 1987, when the country first applied to become a member of the European Community (an economic organization of European countries that in 1992 became the political organization known as the European Union). In March 1995 Turkey was conditionally accepted into a customs union with the EU on the basis that it institute more socially liberal policies.

Words to Understand in This Chapter

diaspora—a dispersion of people who have left their homeland to live in other parts of the world.
smuggle—to move someone or something from one country to another illegally.

Soon afterward, the Turkish government antagonized the EU by sending thousands of troops into northern Iraq to destroy PKK bases. Tensions between Europe and Turkey remained high until the final Turkish military forces withdrew from Iraq a few months later.

The EU particularly criticized Turkey's treatment of Kurdish politicians. In 1994, seven Kurdish members of Turkey's National Assembly were arrested and charged with endangering national security. Four were sentenced to 15 years for "separatist speech," that is, advocating a separate Kurdish state. Among the jailed leaders was one of the first women elected to Turkey's National Assembly, Leyla Zana. A dedicated activist for Kurdish rights, Zana has won several international peace awards.

The European Court of Human Rights condemned the Zana trial in 2001, and three years later, as a result of reforms passed by the Turkish legislature to gain EU approval, the case went to retrial. A 2004 decision by Turkey's State Security Court condemned the four Kurdish deputies to remain behind bars, casting a negative light on the government's progress regarding political reforms. However, the next month the Turkish government abolished the state security courts, and on June 14, 2004, an appeals court overturned the convictions of Zana and three other imprisoned Kurdish deputies. Following her release, she publicly urged Turkish Kurd activists to use nonviolent tactics. Zana was again sentenced to jail time in 2008, 2009, and 2012, each time for allegedly acting on behalf of the PKK. However, higher courts overturned each conviction.

In 1998 the European Union charged Turkey to make drastic improvements in its treatment of the Kurdish people in order to be considered for membership in the EU. Turkey finally succumbed to the pressure, and in 2002 and 2003 the government approved laws granting more civil rights for Kurds. The rise of a reformist political party, the Justice and Development Party (AKP), in November 2002, also had a major impact on the advancement of Kurds' rights.

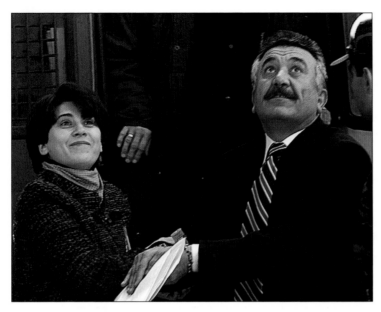

Former Kurdish deputies to Turkey's parliament Leyla Zana and Selim Sadak arrive in handcuffs at their retrial in Ankara, November 2003. European countries denounced Turkey for imprisoning Zana and other deputies in 1994. In June 2004, the Turkish government overturned the sentences of Zana and three others. Since then, Zana has received three other controversial sentences, but each conviction has been overturned.

Among the reforms was the approval of teaching Kurdish in private schools. However, Kurdish classes faced bureaucratic hurdles, and proved too expensive for many Kurds. In 2004, the state-run television broadcaster TRT aired a Kurdish-language program for the first time. TRT launched an all-Kurdish-language channel in 2009 and a radio station soon after.

IRAQI AND TURKISH KURDS AND THE UNITED STATES

Relations between Iraqi Kurds and the U.S. government have ranged from excellent to poor, as the United States has both supported and abandoned the Kurdish people. In the mid-1970s, the Iraqi Kurds felt particularly betrayed. At that time, Iraqi Kurds had requested help against Saddam Hussein's regime. At first the United States worked with the Kurds by providing military support through Iran. But then the pro-West leader of Iran, Shah Mohammad Reza Pahlavi, signed the Algiers Accord with Saddam Hussein, prompting the United States to change its policy. Because Iran was a U.S. ally and had come to terms with Saddam, the United States dropped its support of the Iraqi Kurds. Thousands were left to face the fury of Saddam as his Baathist forces entered northern Iraq and took vengeance on the rebellious Kurds.

The shifting alliances between Iran and the United States have further complicated matters involving Iraqi Kurds. In the early 1970s, the United States was allied with Iran and willing to go along with the decisions made by its government under the shah. However, by the end of the decade Iran's constitutional monarchy had been replaced by the Islamic Republic of Iran, a government that the United States strongly opposed.

Political alliances have also affected the Kurds living in Turkey. For many decades, U.S. leaders have considered Turkey a valuable ally. It is the only Muslim nation that is a member of the North American Treaty Organization, or NATO (a group of allied Western nations). Turkey was often looked to as a barricade against Saddam's regime in Iraq and, since the 1980s, the Islamic government of Iran. Accordingly, the U.S. government has not publicly criticized Turkey over Kurdish human rights violations or pressured its leaders to pass reforms that benefit the Kurds. In addition, the United States has stood by Turkey in its battles against Kurdish rebels. Washington identifies the PKK and its offshoots as terrorist organizations.

While the European Union's sympathy for the Kurds' plight is a source of comfort for the Turkish Kurds, many feel anger toward the United States for overlooking Turkey's repression of the Kurdish people. The Kurds of Iraq, on the other hand, tend to have a positive attitude toward Americans, mostly because of the protection provided by the no-fly zone following the Persian Gulf War in 1991, and their political gains since the 2003 invasion. They do not dwell on the betrayals of the 1970s and the inaction of the 1980s, when the United States and other Western nations did not respond to reports of Kurdish genocides in Iraq. Iran and Iraq were at war, and the United States aided Saddam Hussein because he opposed the Islamic Republic.

Kurdish leaders pressed the United Nations and Western governments after the massacres in 1983 and the Anfal campaign in 1988, pleading for action and support. But despite the Kurdish genocide in northern Iraq, Western nations took no action for more than a decade.

POLITICAL PAWNS

Turkey, Iran, Iraq, and Syria have had shifting alliances among themselves, often because of issues related to the Kurds. At various

After Saddam Hussein attacked the Kurds of northern Iraq in 1991, the United States and its allies established a "no-fly zone" over the northern part of the country, to prevent future aggression by the dictator. Here, an American F-15 flies a routine patrol over snow-covered mountains in northern Iraq, 1999. The no-fly zone existed until the spring of 2003.

times governments have gained advantage by playing the Kurds of neighboring countries against their governments. For example, a dispute with Turkey over the loss of the Hatay province in 1939 made Syria a longtime supporter of Turkey's Kurdish rebels, the PKK. After 1976, when Syrian troops occupied Lebanon, the PKK was permitted to run a training base there. And during the 1990s PKK leaders operated out of Damascus, Syria's capital. However, in a move to improve its relations with Turkey, Syria expelled the rebels in 1998.

Turkey and Iran were also at odds before 1992. Turkey accused Iran of providing support to PKK rebels by allowing them to establish bases in Iran near the Turkish borders. But the establishment of the no-fly zone and the creation of the Kurdistan Regional Government in Iraq concerned both countries. Iran believed that Iraqi Kurdistan had become a sanctuary for Iranian opposition groups, and in 1993 the Iranian government sided with Turkey in opposing the creation of any kind of independent Kurdish state in Iraq. Syria also declared the belief that Iraq should remain intact as one state.

EFFECTS OF THE 2003 PERSIAN GULF WAR

Following the 2003 war, Iraqi Kurdistan's neighbors looked to the region with great concern. The countries of Syria, Iran, and Turkey feared that the creation of a Kurdish state in Iraq would inspire Kurds in their countries to break away and form a separate state. Turkey threatened to invade if Iraqi Kurds declared independence, and it insisted that the Kurds had no rightful claim to the oil-rich cities of Kirkuk and Mosul. Of the three ethnic groups in Iraq, the Kurds had been most supportive of the U.S. action in Iraq, contributing *peshmerga* commandos and fighters to U.S. forces during the war and later in battles against insurgents. Most Iraqi Kurds welcomed the overthrow of Saddam, and unlike inhabitants to the south, felt no hostility to the fewer than 300 coalition troops who were based in Iraqi Kurdistan.

In the years following the invasion, some Kurds' opinions shifted due to the perception that coalition forces had broken promises—for example, a referendum on KRG control of Kirkuk was repeatedly postponed. However, the U.S. and the Kurds have recently found themselves united in the mission of opposing the Islamic State in Iraq. The U.S. has supplied *peshmerga* fighters and carried out air strikes on ISIL targets in coordination with the Kurdish army.

Although currently preoccupied with the conflict with ISIL, neighboring countries still look to Iraqi Kurdistan with some apprehension. It now seems an autonomous Kurdish region in Syria may fulfill and increase fears about the spread of Kurdish independence. However, these nations may also pursue opportunities presented by Kurdish control. For example, Turkish companies have made a profit rebuilding the infrastructure in the KRG.

An Iraq that remains united requires that Arabs, Turkomen, and Kurds, groups that for centuries have fought bitterly among themselves, live together in peace and unite against militants such as ISIL. Before ISIL seized land in northwest Iraq in 2014, the KRG region had become one of the most secure areas of the country. Even now residents enjoy more safety than in other parts of Iraq where the Islamic State rules or where the weak central government is unable to maintain security. However, there have been a few ISIL attacks in the KRG, such as an attack against the Security Directorate in Erbil.

The *peshmerga* successes against ISIL, including the KRG control of Kirkuk, have strengthened the independence plans of KRG president Massoud Barzani and other Kurdish leaders. However, most outside analysts say that an independent Kurdish state is still unlikely. Iraqi Kurds will need to address their dual identities in a changing country.

A DIVIDED PEOPLE

Many political analysts believe that the Kurds have not been able to achieve power as a united ethnic group because tribal loyalty has stifled development of a Kurdish national loyalty. In the past, Kurds living in different countries have pledged allegiance to their regional tribes rather than to a united Kurdish nation. Turkish Kurds have fought Iraqi Kurds, who have fought Iranian Kurds.

This division has extended to how Kurds react to conflicts involving Kurdish groups and their respective governments. For example, Iraqi Kurdish leaders cooperated with the Turkish government in attempting to flush out PKK members based in northern Iraq. The PKK, in turn, has sharply criticized Iraqi Kurdish leaders and has promoted anti-Kurdish Regional Government prop-

United Nations Secretary-General Ban Ki-moon (right) meets with Mohammed Fuad Masum, the president of Iraq. Masum is a Kurd who was born in the city of Koy Sanjaq, near Erbil; he succeeded Jalal Talabani as president of Iraq in 2014.

U.S. president Barack Obama meets with Masoud Barzani, president of Iraqi Kurdistan, in the Oval Office.

aganda through the pro-PKK television station, Medya. Such broadcasts have helped drive a wedge between Turkish and Iraqi Kurds.

At times, the complex relationships among Kurds, opposition parties, and host countries become a confusing puzzle. For instance, the government of Iran is said to support Ansar al-Islam, the radical Islamic group that has fought against the PUK. However, the PUK also has good relations with Iran, even though the PUK allows the Kurdish Democratic Party of Iran (KDPI), which opposes the Iranian government, to operate in northern Iraq. Iranian agents have also been granted permission to enter PUK territory in exchange for diplomatic, economic, and military aid from the Iranian government.

In addition to this environment of shifting alliances, significant language differences divide Kurds. There is no standardized written language, as Iraqi and Iranian Kurds use the Arabic alphabet while Turkish Kurds use the Roman.

In countries such as Iran and Turkey, where large numbers of Kurds have assimilated into their nation's respective societies, the Kurdish identity is not as strong as it used to be. In Turkey, many Kurds denied their origins to get ahead in business or the government, or to simply get a job. In both Iran and Turkey, many in the younger generation do not know how to speak Kurdish at all.

UNITING KURDS WITH TECHNOLOGY

Around 1990, satellite television, which allows programs to be beamed all over the world, provided the first means for Kurds to share their message of nationalism with other Kurds, both inside Kurdistan and in Europe. A station licensed in Britain, the Kurdish Satellite Channel, brought the Kurdish language, map, and national anthem to Turkey and other parts of Kurdistan. Because such broadcasts were prohibited, Turkish government soldiers were sent out to destroy satellite dishes. The Iranian government also protested against the broadcasts. But the satellite television network remained a powerful tool for spreading and strengthening Kurdish nationalism.

"I knew a family in Turkey," explained Kurdish researcher and University of Toronto professor Amir Hassanpour to Salon.com in April 2004. "They never believed they'd be able to see Kurdish on television, but when they saw the shows, they changed their mind. They believed the Kurdish nation could exist."

Today, language barriers are breaking down as television and radio announcers broadcast in Kermanji and Sorani. For about $100, Kurdish families can purchase a digital receiver and a satellite dish that provides access to Kurdish channels. A television set can be found in the homes of even the poorest Kurds.

Similarly, the Internet has allowed the culture of Kurdistan to

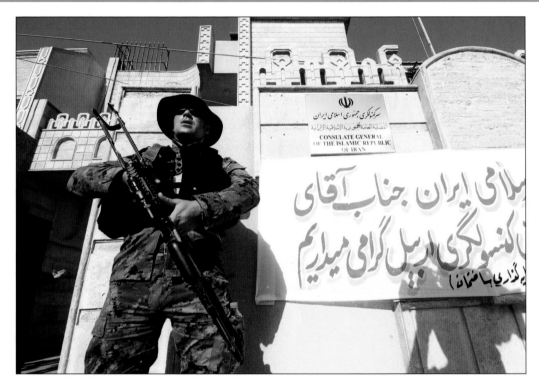

A Kurdish soldier stands guard outside the Iranian consulate in Erbil, Iraq. The *peshmerga* have been the most successful of the ground forces fighting ISIL in Iraq and Syria.

grow in cyberspace. Kurds in different countries can talk with one another through blogs and chat rooms. A variety of Kurdish websites educate Kurds and other people about the Kurdish language, history, music, and culture, as well as provide up-to-the-minute news coverage on issues of concern to Kurds. Many sites are named for the Kurdish nation, such as Kurdland.com, Kurdistan.net, and Kurdishmedia.com. Some media analysts refer to Kurdistan as a cyber-state—that is, a nation that exists online, if not in reality.

Through the Internet, Kurds in Turkey or Syria—countries that censored Kurdish publications—received news of the progress of the fledgling government in northern Iraq. When Iraq's interim constitution was signed in March 2004, with its guarantees of continued autonomy for Iraqi Kurdistan, Kurds in Iran and Syria celebrated with public rallies. Syrian demonstrators carried portraits of Kurdish leaders, notably Massoud Barzani of Iraq's KDP and Abdullah Öcalan, the jailed leader of the PKK.

That same month Internet reports about the clashes between Kurds and Arab police in Syria and reports of government violence against demonstrators quickly reached Kurds throughout the rest of the world. Many ethnic Kurds living in Europe and Iraq immediately took to the streets, demonstrating in support. Kurds in Iraq also marched in Erbil, where they called on the United Nations and human rights groups to end Syrian oppression of the Kurds.

Although they may not always understand each other's dialects, most Kurds believe they are united by their shared history of suffering and oppression. And as the Internet lifts barriers in communication—an issue that in the past has divided Kurds and reinforced tribal loyalty instead of national loyalty—Kurds may come closer to founding their own state. As the Internet gives Kurds around the world a way of connecting, it strengthens the nation of Kurdistan, making it an idea that could become a reality.

 ## Text-Dependent Questions

1. What region has the largest population of Kurds outside Kurdistan?
2. How has the European Union influenced improvements in Kurdish rights in Turkey?
3. Describe the relationship between Iraqi Kurds and the United States.

 ## Research Project

Use the Internet or a library to learn more about the Kurdish diaspora to Europe and North America. Create an outline for a report with sections for Reasons for Leaving Kurdistan, Ways of Integrating into a Foreign Society, and Ways of Preserving Kurdish Culture. Fill in the outline with details from your research.

1918   British troops occupy the predominantly Kurdish and oil-rich Ottoman *vilayet* (province) of Mosul.

1920   The Treaty of Sevres that ends World War I dissolves the Ottoman Empire and promises the creation of the independent nation of Kurdistan.

1923   The Treaty of Lausanne supercedes the Treaty of Sevres and establishes Turkey as independent nation with claims to part of Kurdistan; the newly created nations of Iraq and Syria also include parts of the Kurdish homeland; Sheikh Mahmoud Barzinji incites uprising against the British, establishing Kurdish kingdom in northern Iraq that is overthrown by British forces the following year.

1932   A second Kurdish uprising, led by Mulla Mustafa Barzani and his older brother, Ahmad, is crushed.

1943   Mustafa Barzani leads another uprising and gains control over parts of Erbil and Badinan.

1946   Iraqi Kurdish rebels are defeated by the British, who drive them into Iran; Iraqi Kurds join Iranian Kurds, led by Qazi Mohamed, in establishing the independent Mahabad Republic, which falls in early 1947; the Kurdistan Democratic Party (KDP) is founded by Mustafa Barzani with the goal of creating an independent Kurdistan.

1958   The Iraqi monarch is overthrown; a new Iraqi constitution promises Kurdish rights.

1961   Barzani leads northern Iraqi Kurds in revolt against the dictatorship of President Abd al-Karim Qasim. Although defeated, the Kurds continue sporadic fighting; Syrian census strips 200,000 Kurds of their citizenship.

1970   Kurds are granted some self-rule and representation in Iraqi government.

1974   The KDP rejects Iraqi government autonomy agreement over land disputes; the KDP (with funding from the United States and Iran) attacks Iraqi government.

1975   Iraqi Kurdish uprising is crushed after the United States and the shah of Iran remove their support; Jalal Talabani breaks away from KDP and forms the Patriotic Union of Kurdistan (PUK).

1978   In Turkey, Abdullah Öcalan helps found the Kurdistan Workers Party (PKK).

1979   KDP leader Mustafa Barzani dies and is replaced by his son Massoud; Iranian Kurds revolt during Islamic revolution in Iran.

1980–88   Iraqi Kurds side with Iranian forces during the Iran-Iraq War.

1988   Towards the end of the Iran-Iraq war, Saddam Hussein's *Anfal* campaign kills thousands of Kurds and forces another 1.5 million into exile; thousands of civilians die in poison gas attacks on villages, including Halabja.

1991 A 34-member U.N. coalition enters into Persian Gulf War against Saddam Hussein; Kurds rise up against the Iraqi government at war's end but are crushed; coalition forces help refugees and set up no-fly zone in northern Iraq.

1992 Turkish military forces enter Iraq to attack PKK bases; elections are held in Iraqi Kurdistan.

1993 Martial law is imposed in southeastern Turkey.

1994 In Iraq, the KDP and PUK begin four years of fighting for control of the Kurdish autonomous region.

1995 Turkish troops enter Iraq to destroy PKK bases.

1996 KDP sides with Saddam Hussein's Iraqi army against PUK.

1998 PUK and KDP sign peace agreement.

1999 Öcalan is captured and convicted of treason; his death sentence is later reduced to life imprisonment; terrorist attacks follow his capture and trial.

2001 Fighting breaks out between the PUK and the Islamic fundamentalist group Jund al-Islam, later renamed Ansar al-Islam.

2002 Kurdish regional parliament reconvenes in Erbil after a six-year interruption.

2003 On March 20, U.S.-led coalition forces invade Iraq; in April, U.S. forces advance into Baghdad and take control of Kirkuk and Mosul with the help of Kurdish fighters; the U.S.-appointed Iraqi Governing Council (IGC), which includes several Kurdish leaders, meets in July.

2004 In February, over 100 people, including senior politicians, die in suicide bombing at PUK and KDP offices in Erbil; the IGC approves interim constitution promising autonomy for Iraqi Kurdistan; in June, the new Iraqi Interim Government, which includes a Kurdish vice president, replaces the IGC.

2005 Police violently break up a Kurdish pro-citizenship demonstration in Damascus. In April, Iraq elects National Assembly, which votes Jalal Talabani president; permanent Iraqi constitution is ratified.

2006 Former Iraqi dictator Saddam Hussein stands trial for 1980s military campaigns that killed about 100,000 Kurds, and is executed in December; attacks targeting Yezidis in northern Iraq kill at least 300.

2007   About 50 Turkish soldiers and civilians die in October in attacks by the outlawed PKK; Turkey launches air strikes in northern Iraq targeting the PKK.

2008   In February, Turkey's military enters Iraqi Kurdistan; 153 PKK operatives and nineteen Turkish soldiers are killed. In December, suicide bombers kill 55 people at a Kirkuk restaurant, during a meeting of Kurdish and Arab leaders.

2009   Kirkuk and the three Kurdish provinces do not participate in Iraqi municipal elections on January 31; President Talabani states that a fully autonomous Iraqi Kurdistan is unlikely. Turkey announces plans for an official Kurdish-language translation of the Qur'an.

2009   A Kurdish-language state-sponsored television and radio station are launched in Turkey.

2010   A young Turkish Kurd is shot after an argument about singing Kurdish songs in a bar. Turkey bombs suspected PKK hideouts in Iraq.

2011   Thousands of Syrian Kurds are granted citizenship. A Syrian Kurdish activist is assassinated and Kurds blame President al Assad's regime. Kurdish militants kill 24 Turkish soldiers in a PKK area near the Iraq border.

2012   The Turkish government begins peace talks with the PKK. Syrian security forces retreat from Kurdish areas, leaving them under local control.

2013   Three Kurdish women are shot in Paris. Abdullah Öcalan, the imprisoned PKK leader, calls for peaceful dialogue between Kurds and the Turkish government. Turkish and Iraqi Kurdistan officials negotiate a deal for an oil pipeline that will carry Kurdish oil into Turkey. The Kurdish region of Syria declares autonomy, taking the name of Rojava or Western Kurdistan.

2014   Islamic State fighters take control of Mosul and refugees flee into Iraqi Kurdistan. KRG peshmerga fighters recover Kirkuk from ISIL and claim the city as part of the KRG. KRG and Iraqi officials sign an agreement to share oil revenues and to cooperate and share resources in the fight against ISIL.

2015   After nearly four months of fighting, Kurdish soldiers take control of the Syrian city of Kobani from ISIL. The Syrian government agrees to negotiate the conditions of an autonomous Kurdish region. In May, protests erupt in Mahabad, Iran over the sexual assault and suicide of a Kurdish woman; the protests spread to other Kurdish regions and transform into demands for increased Kurdish rights and self-government.

SERIES GLOSSARY

autonomy—the right of self-government.

BCE and CE—an alternative to the traditional Western designation of calendar eras, which used the birth of Jesus as a dividing line. BCE stands for "Before the Common Era," and is equivalent to BC ("Before Christ"). Dates labeled CE, or "Common Era," are equivalent to Anno Domini (AD, or "the Year of Our Lord").

caliphate—an Islamic theocratic state, in which the ruler, or caliph, has authority over both the spiritual and temporal lives of his subjects and all people must obey Islamic laws.

civil society—the sum total of institutions, organizations, and groups promoting social and civic causes in a country (for example, human rights groups, labor unions, arts foundations) that are not funded or controlled by the government or business interests.

colonialism—control or domination by one country over an area or people outside its boundaries; the policy of colonizing foreign lands.

ideology—a system of beliefs, values, and ideas forming the basis of a social, economic, or political philosophy.

Islamist—a Muslim who advocates the reformation of society and government in accordance with Islamic laws and principles.

jihadism—adherence to the idea that Muslims should carry out a war against un-Islamic groups and ideas, especially Westerners and Western liberal culture.

nationalism—the belief that shared ethnicity, language, and history should form the basis for political organization; the desire of people with a common culture to have their own state.

Pan-Arabism—a movement seeking to unite all Arab peoples into a single state.

self-determination—determination by a people of their own future political status.

Sharia—Islamic law, based on the Qur'an and other Islamic writings and traditions. The Sharia sets forth the moral goals of an Islamic society, and governs a Muslim's religious political, social, and private life.

Shia—the smaller of Islam's two major branches, whose rift with the larger Sunni branch originated in seventh-century disputes over who should succeed the prophet Muhammad as leader of the Muslim community.

Sunni—a Muslim who belongs to the largest branch of Islam.

Wahhabism—a highly conservative form of Sunni Islam practiced in Saudi Arabia.

Zionism—the movement to establish a Jewish state in Palestine; support for the State of Israel.

Bird, Christiane. *A Thousand Sighs, A Thousand Revolts: Journeys in Kurdistan.* New York: Ballantine Books, 2004.

Bulloch, John, and Harvey Morris. *No Friends but the Mountains: The Tragic History of the Kurds.* New York: Oxford University Press, 1992.

Chaliand, Gerard, ed. *A People Without a Country: The Kurds and Kurdistan.* Trans. Michael Pallis. New York: Olive Branch Press, 1993.

Gibson, Bryan R. *Sold Out? US Foreign Policy, Iraq, the Kurds, and the Cold War.* Palgrave Macmillan, 2015.

Gunter, Michael M., and Mohammed M.A. Ahmed. *The Kurdish Spring: Geopolitical Changes and the Kurds.* Costa Mesa, Calif: Mazda Publishers, 2013.

Hokayem, Emile. *Syria's Uprising and the Fracturing of the Levant.* London: International Institute for Strategic Studies, 2014.

Lawrence, Quil. *Invisible Nation: How the Kurds' Quest for Statehood Is Shaping Iraq and the Middle East.* New York: Walker & Company, 2008.

McMeekin, Sean. *The Ottoman Endgame: War, Revolution, and the Making of the Modern Middle East.* New York: Penguin Press, 2015.

Mansfield, Peter. *A History of the Middle East.* 4th ed. revised and updated by Nicholas Pelham. New York: Penguin Books, 2013.

Marcus, Aliza. *Blood and Belief: The PKK and the Kurdish Fight for Independence.* New York and London: New York University Press, 2007.

Saleem, Hiner, trans. Catherine Temerson. *My Father's Rifle: A Childhood in Kurdistan.* New York: Farrar, Straus and Giroux, 2005.

Schwedler, Jillian. *Understanding the Contemporary Middle East.* Boulder, Colo.: Lynne Rienner Publishers, 2013.

Sekulow, Jay. *Rise of ISIS: A Threat We Can't Ignore.* New York: Howard Books, 2014.

Stern, Jessica, and J.M. Berger. *ISIS: The State of Terror.* New York: Ecco, 2015.

INTERNET RESOURCES

http://cabinet.gov.krd

The official website of the government of Iraqi Kurdistan provides news and information about government programs and activities.

https://www.cia.gov/library/publications/the-world-factbook

The CIA World Factbook website provides a great deal of statistical information about the countries where most Kurds live: Iran, Iraq, Syria, and Turkey. The World Factbook is updated regularly.

www.mideasti.org

An extensive resource geared to educate Americans about the Middle East. This academic site includes loads of information for research.

www.un.org/english

The English-language web page for the United Nations can be searched for Kurdistan-related stories and information.

www.bbc.com/news

The official website of BBC News provides articles and videos on important international news and events related to the Middle East and elsewhere.

www.aljazeera.com

The English-language website of the Arabic news service Al Jazeera provides articles and videos on breaking news, as well as feature stories that provide background material, including profiles of leaders and essays reacting to major events.

www.fpri.org

The website of the Foreign Policy Research Institute includes informative essays by FPRI scholars on events in the Middle East.

Numbers in ***bold italic*** refer to captions.

INDEX

INDEX

PICTURE CREDITS

Senior Consultant CAMILLE PECASTAING, PH.D., is acting director of the Middle East Studies Program at the Paul H. Nitze School of Advanced International Studies at Johns Hopkins University. A student of behavioral sciences and historical sociology, Dr. Pecastaing's research focuses on the cognitive and emotive foundations of xenophobic political cultures and ethnoreligious violence, using the Muslim world and its European and Asian peripheries as a case study. He has written on political Islam, Islamist terrorism, social change, and globalization. Pecastaing's essays have appeared in many journals, including *World Affairs* and *Policy Review*. He is the author of *Jihad in the Arabian Sea* (Hoover Institution Press, 2011).

The FOREIGN POLICY RESEARCH INSTITUTE (FPRI) provided editorial guidance for this series. FPRI is one of the nation's oldest "think tanks." The Institute's Middle East Program focuses on Gulf security, monitors the Arab-Israeli peace process, and sponsors an annual conference for teachers on the Middle East, plus periodic briefings on key developments in the region.

Among FPRI's trustees are a former Undersecretary of Defense, a former Secretary of the Navy, a former Assistant Secretary of State, a foundation president, and numerous active or retired corporate CEOs, lawyers, and civic leaders. Scholars affiliated with FPRI include a Pulitzer Prize–winning historian; a former president of Swarthmore College; a Bancroft Prize–winning historian; and a former Ambassador and senior staff member of the National Security Council. And FPRI counts among its extended network of scholars—especially its Inter-University Study Groups—representatives of many diverse disciplines, including political science, history, economics, law, management, religion, sociology, and psychology.

LEEANNE GELLETLY is a freelance writer and editor living outside Philadelphia. She has worked in publishing for more than 20 years and has written on a variety of subjects. Her books include the biographies *Harriet Beecher Stowe* and *Mae Jemison*; geography titles that explore Bolivia, Colombia, Somalia, and Turkey; and books on social issues such as Mexican immigration and violence in the media.